PERSPECTIVES ON EARLY CHILDHOOD PSYCHOLOGY AND EDUCATION

SPECIAL FOCUSES

Family Collaboration in

Early Childhood Education

and

Research in Community

Childcare Programs

Volume 3, Issue 2
Fall 2018

Copyright © 2018
Pace University Press
41 Park Row
15th floor
New York, NY 10038

ISBN: 978-0-9619518-9-4
ISSN: 2471-1527

Member

Council of Editors of Learned Journals

EDITOR
Vincent C. Alfonso, *Gonzaga University*

SPECIAL FOCUSES EDITORS
Stacy L. Bender, *University of Massachusetts Boston*
Angel Fettig, *Washington University*
Adrienne Garro, *Kean University*
Keri Giordano, *Kean University*

EDITORIAL REVIEW BOARD
Vincent C. Alfonso, *Gonzaga University*
Stephen Bagnato, *University of Pittsburgh*
Renee Bergeron, *Consultant*
Zeynep Biringen, *Colorado State University*
Bruce Bracken, *College of William & Mary*
Melissa Bray, *University of Connecticut*
Victoria Comerchero, *Touro College*
Gerard Costa, *Montclair State University*
Grace Elizade-Utnick, *City University of New York at Brooklyn College*
Nancy Evangelista, *Alfred University*
Kathryn Fletcher, *Ball State University*
Randy Floyd, *University of Memphis*
Gilbert Foley, *New York Center for Child Development*
Laurie Ford, *University of British Columbia*
Pamela Guess, *University of Tennessee*
Robin Hojnoski, *Lehigh University*
Tammy Hughes (Associate Editor), *Duquesne University*
Paul McCabe, *Brooklyn College*
Sara McCane-Bowling, *University of Tennessee*
David McIntosh (Associate Editor), *Ball State University*
Barbara A. Mowder (Associate Editor), *Pace University*
Geraldine Oades-Sese, *Rutgers Robert Wood Johnson Medical School*
Matt Reynolds, *University of Kansas*
Gail Ross, *NY Presbyterian Hospital*
Flo Rubinson (Associate Editor), *Brooklyn College*
Susan Ruby, *Eastern Washington University*
Mark Sossin, *Pace University*
Esther Stavrou, *Yeshiva University*
Mark Terjesen, *St. John's University*
Lea Theodore, *College of William and Mary*
Mary Ward, *Weill Cornell Medical College*
Adriana Wissel, *Gonzaga University*

TABLE OF CONTENTS

Editor's Note 1
Vincent C. Alfonso

SPECIAL FOCUS I: FAMILY COLLABORATION IN EARLY CHILDHOOD EDUCATION

Introduction to the Special Focus: Family Collaboration in Early Childhood Special Education............................... 5
Stacy L. Bender and Angel Fettig

Family-School Partnership in Positive Behavior Interventions and Supports in an Early Childhood Center 9
Sarah Fefer, Marina Donnelly, Kayla Gordon, and Robin Fernandes

Implementing Family Education Programs in Preschool Settings 35
Stacy L. Bender and Sarah Fefer

Coaching Families to Promote Social Emotional Competence and Address Challenging Behaviors for Young Children with Disabilities 59
Angel Fettig, Erin E. Barton, and Hedda Meadan

Effectiveness and Usability of a Self-Administered Parent Training Intervention for Building Social-Emotional Competence Among at Risk Preschoolers............................... 77
Rebecca N. Thomson and John S. Carlson

SPECIAL FOCUS II: RESEARCH IN COMMUNITY CHILDCARE PROGRAMS

Introduction to the Special Focus: Research in Community Childcare Programs.. 99
Keri Giordano and Adrienne Garro

Intentional Leadership: Utilizing Communities of Practice & Coaching Intervention to Support Professional Development of Early Childhood Program Administrators 103
Keri Giordano, Arlene Martin, and Kim M. Cornell

Factors Associated with Global Quality Change in Infant and Toddler Child Care Programs 125
Maegan Lokteff and Ann Berghout Austin

Exploring Culture, Race, and Ethnicity in Early Childhood Mental Health Consultation: The Role of the Consultative Alliance .. 149
Anna E. Davis, Eva Marie Shivers, and Deborah F. Perry

Knowledge and Perceptions Related to Evidence-Based Behavioral Interventions Among Early Childhood Educators 173
Adrienne Garro, Rachel Pess, and Nicolette Rittenhouse-Young

LIST OF CONTRIBUTORS 199

EDITORIAL POLICY 203

CALL FOR PAPERS 205

Editor's Note

In this, my last issue as editor of *Perspectives on Early Childhood Psychology and Education* (PECPE), I am pleased to introduce for the first time two special focuses. The first special focus is *Family Collaboration in Early Childhood Special Education*, guest-edited by Drs. Stacy L. Bender and Angel Fettig. Manuscripts in this special focus address family engagement and interventions to improve young children's behavior and overall educational experience. The second special focus is *Research in Community Childcare Programs*, guest-edited by Drs. Keri Giordano and Adrienne Garro. These editors include manuscripts that address the unique and oftentimes misunderstood needs of early childhood educators and other professionals who work with community childcare programs or centers. Drs. Giordano and Garro make the case that working or collaborating with community programs is significantly different than working or collaborating with state-funded programs or centers.

As stated above, this is my last issue as editor of PECPE. I have had a great learning experience launching this new journal and making contributions to early childhood psychology and education. I am especially grateful to Associate Editors Drs. Tammy Hughes, David McIntosh, Barbara Mowder, and Florence Rubinson for their tenacious efforts in moving us from the *Journal of Early Childhood and Infant Psychology* (JECIP) to PECPE, excellent reviews of manuscripts, and general support of the editorial practices and policies of PECPE. I am also grateful to the 25+ editorial review board members, many of whom continued to review manuscripts after JECIP was no longer viable. I could not have been successful without the consistent support of Manuela Soares, Director of Pace University Press (PUP), her staff including the new Associate Director of PUP, Dr. Stephanie Hsu. Finally, but certainly not least, I would like to acknowledge Gina Frerichs, Jaleh Davari, and Claire Seeger for their time, encouragement, and editorial support these past five years.

I am delighted to announce that Dr. David McIntosh is the new editor of PECPE beginning with the Spring 2019 issue. Dr. McIntosh has myriad years of editorial experience, including being an Associate Editor of JECIP and PECPE for nearly 10 years. I can think of few individuals better than Dr. McIntosh to take over the reins of PECPE and I look forward to his editorship of the journal.

We are interested in proposals for a special focus for the spring 2019 issue and any general manuscripts as well. Information regarding submission of manuscripts is found in the call for papers. Readers who are interested in becoming a member of the editorial review board of *Perspectives* should contact Dr. McIntosh via email at demcintosh@bsu.edu. In closing we hope you find *Perspectives* to be a useful journal in your research and practice. Please feel free to contact us with ideas, comments, and suggestions. We are very open to innovative ideas and look forward to hearing from you.

Enjoy *Perspectives*!
Vincent C. Alfonso, Editor

SPECIAL FOCUS I

Family Collaboration in Early Childhood Education

Introduction to the Special Focus: Family Collaboration in Early Childhood Special Education

Stacy L. Bender and Angel Fettig

Family collaboration is essential for children's behavioral and academic success in school, and pre-kindergarten is an optimal time to promote and nurture school-parent relationships (Powell, Son, File, & San Juan, 2010). For parents of young children experiencing developmental, behavioral, social, academic, and cognitive difficulties, parent engagement is particularly important as research has shown that children with disabilities experience more favorable outcomes when parents are involved in intervention implementation (LeBel, Chafouleas, Britner, & Simonsen, 2012). Additionally, family involvement and intervention is a required component of the Individuals with Disabilities Education Act for young children with disabilities or at-risk for disabilities. Engaging families in intervention implementation improves parents' understanding, implementation, and participation in interventions, thus leading to increased learning opportunities at home, generalizability of skills learned in school to the home environment, and enhanced skills related to parenting.

This special focus of *Perspectives on Early Childhood Psychology and Education (PECPE)* is Family Collaboration in Early Childhood Special Education and centers on various collaboration and engagement practices targeting families of preschool-age students with disabilities or those at-risk for disabilities in the future. Family engagement frameworks and the usability (i.e., acceptable, feasible) and evidence-informed interventions for engaging families in the intervention process (i.e., planning, implementation) and ensuring integrity of implementation are discussed.

There are several exciting and unique features about the articles included in this special focus. All the articles included describe various methods of family engagement and interventions that have been found to be effective, yet as the authors indicate, are implemented with limited frequency. To improve the quality and quantity of implementation, the articles provide practical and feasible strategies and suggestions for how researchers and practitioners can implement these interventions in their settings for families. Emphasis of adaptation for families' diverse and unique needs and the theme of considering each of the strategies and interventions across universal, secondary, and tertiary levels are discussed throughout each of the articles.

Fefer, Donnelly, Gordon, and Fernandes present a case study that describes and provides examples of family-school partnership efforts within a multi-tiered framework of behavioral support in an integrated preschool. The researchers and preschool that were actively implementing Positive Behavior Interventions and Supports (PBIS) were focused on ways to enhance family-school partnership and align these practices with the core elements of PBIS (i.e., data, systems, practices). Practical family engagement strategies at multiple tiers are provided and considerations are discussed.

Bender and Fefer describe the rationale and benefits of implementing parent education programs in public preschools. Using an implementation science framework, they describe steps practitioners and researchers could feasibly go through when exploring, selecting, implementing, and evaluating the outcomes of parent education programs. The researchers discuss their own experiences in implementing parent education programs and considerations to make when adapting for various parent populations.

Fettig, Barton, and Meadan discuss family coaching and 10 evidence-informed family coaching practices that are empirically supported. These strategies are described to understand how practitioners can partner with families and how family coaching can be used as a home-based support to addressing challenging behavior for young children. A brief case example is provided to illustrate the practices and additional considerations when implementing family coaching.

Carlson and Thomson implemented and evaluated the usability and effectiveness of the Devereux Early Childhood Assessment, Second Edition family guide. This self-administered parent training intervention that targets social-emotional competence for at-risk preschool students was found to have high usability amongst parents. Additionally, improvements in social-emotional competence were found for some but not all students. The article discusses ways to increase effectiveness for families and other considerations needed when working with families and their unique needs.

Given the important and positive outcomes found for children and families, we hope this special issue continues to further understanding of feasible and adaptable practice efforts, and inform future research of effective ways to improve family engagement for preschool children with disabilities.

References

LeBel, T. J., Chafouleas, S. M., Britner, P. A., & Simonsen, B. (2012). Using a daily report card in an intervention package involving home-school communication to reduce disruptive behavior in preschoolers. *Journal of Positive Behavior Interventions, 15*, 103–112. doi:10.1177/1098300712440451

Powell, D. R., Son, S. H., File, N., & San Juan, R. R. (2010). Parent-school relationships and children's academic and social outcomes in public school pre-kindergarten. *Journal of School Psychology, 48*, 269–292. doi:10.1016/j.jsp.2010.03.002

Family-School Partnership in Positive Behavior Interventions and Supports in an Early Childhood Center

*Sarah Fefer, Marina Donnelly,
Kayla Gordon, and Robin Fernandes*

Abstract

Although research supports the implementation of Positive Behavior Interventions and Supports (PBIS) in home and school settings for young children, little attention has been given to methods for partnering with families within PBIS in early childhood centers. This may be particularly important given the benefits of early intervention for young children and because early family-school partnership efforts may set the stage for ongoing family engagement in their child's schooling. A case study from one early childhood center is presented with examples of family-school partnership efforts organized within the core PBIS elements of data, systems, and practices. These elements can serve as a skeleton upon which individual early childhood settings can build their own unique tools and resources to encourage family-school partnership within PBIS, accounting for the needs and strengths of the specific populations they serve. It is imperative that early childhood settings strategize around how to best engage families in their behavioral and social-emotional programming, and the examples provided are meant to inspire this process with a focus on data, systems, and practices. PBIS serves as a natural framework to engage families in partnering with schools to promote their child's success.

***Keywords*: family engagement, PBIS, early childhood, preschool, family-school partnership**

Challenging behavior is common among young children, with 17.4% of a representative sample of children under 5 displaying high rates of externalizing behaviors (Holtz, Fox, & Meurer, 2015). This is particularly problematic as challenging behavior in preschool has been shown to predict more serious problems later in childhood and adolescence (McCabe & Frede, 2007). Efforts to resolve challenging behavior are most effective when parents are involved (Epstein et al., 2015). Early childhood educational settings serve as an ideal environment for proactive teaching of behavioral and social-emotional expectations and to establish partnerships between schools and families from the start of each child's academic career. Family engagement is a top priority for many schools with the goal of developing ongoing reciprocal communication between family members and school staff, and with both parties as equal partners to promote student success (Weist, Garbacz, Lane, & Kincaid, 2017). Engaging families in their child's education has been shown to enhance academic and behavioral outcomes across many studies (Fan & Chen, 2001). Additionally, the importance of establishing consistency across home and school settings is supported by both theoretical (Bronfenbrenner, 1977) and experimental work (Garbacz, Sheridan, Kozial, Kwon, & Holmes, 2015). The implementation of multi-tiered frameworks, such as Positive Behavior Interventions and Supports (PBIS) or Response to Intervention (RtI), has been suggested as one method to establish consistent behavioral expectations across home and school settings (Weist et al., 2017) and enhance family support in early childhood centers (McCart et al., 2010).

PBIS is a preventive framework organized around tiers of support to meet the behavioral needs of all students and prevent escalation of challenging behavior (Horner, Sugai, & Anderson, 2010). Three tiers of primary, secondary, and tertiary supports are provided to meet student needs (Sugai & Horner, 2002). Primary (or universal) practices emphasize program-wide and classroom-specific supports, such as explicitly teaching and acknowledging positively stated behavioral expectations. Students who continue to exhibit challenging behaviors despite receiving support at this primary tier are systematically identified for more individualized support. At these secondary and tertiary levels, students receive more frequent teaching of behavioral expectations and more frequent feedback and reinforcement tied to their behavior. Function-based intervention plans are implemented for students who demonstrate a need for individualized supports (Sugai & Horner, 2002). The need for integrated systems, data, and practices is emphasized within PBIS to achieve full implementation across all three tiers with these essential elements working in concert to achieve desired outcomes for schools, students, and families (Weist et al., 2017).

There is a growing body of research supporting the implementation of PBIS with young children in school (e.g., Hemmeter, Fox, Jack, & Broyles, 2007; Jolivette & Steed, 2010; Jolstead et al., 2017; Stanton-Chapman, Walker, Voorhees, & Snell, 2016; Steed, Pomerleau, Muscott, & Rohde, 2013) and at home (e.g., Dunlap, Ester, Langhans, & Fox, 2006; Lucyshyn et al., 2015). These studies have demonstrated positive outcomes related to teacher and parent acceptability of PBIS, ease of implementation, and child on-task and problem behavior in home and at school. However, none of these articles focus directly on family-school partnership within early childhood PBIS. Other authors have considered family engagement (McCart et al., 2010) and parent education (Phaneuf & McIntyre, 2007) in early childhood within three-tiered frameworks, but have not focused on PBIS specifically.

Despite limited research around family partnership and PBIS in early childhood, there is extensive guidance available on applying PBIS principles to early childhood settings available through The Pyramid Model (http://challengingbehavior.cbcs.usf.edu/). This is a multi-tiered framework to organize evidence-based practices to meet the specific needs of early childhood programs, with an emphasis on systems and data-based decision making to promote positive student outcomes (Allen & Steed, 2016; Fox, Dunlap, Hemmeter, Joseph, & Strain, 2003). This model adds two additional universal components to PBIS: nurturing and responsive relationships and high-quality supportive environments (Allen & Steed, 2016; Fox et al., 2003). Although relationships, including parent-teacher relationships, are emphasized explicitly within each tier of this model, there is less guidance available about how to best facilitate family-school partnerships within PBIS for young children (McCart et al., 2010; Reinke, Splett, Robeson, & Offutt, 2009; Weist et al., 2017).

This paper provides examples from one early childhood center that focused specifically on integrating their family-school partnership practices within a PBIS framework. Examples of alignment and integration are organized around the key PBIS elements of systems, data, and practices (see Figure 1) to emphasize the focus on prevention for young children and to highlight that planning and implementation efforts should be divided equitably among these three elements to enhance positive outcomes for children and families. Previous work related to family engagement in PBIS is organized primarily around practices across each tier of support, with less emphasis on systems and data-based decision making (see Weist et al., 2017). PBIS and family-school partnership are not two separate initiatives; rather, we recognize and aim to accentuate natural alignment and emphasize that family partnership can strengthen PBIS efforts across all three key elements of implementation. To illustrate that partnering with families fits organically within a PBIS framework, the sections below contain examples of specific systems, data, and practices from an early childhood center to show an alliance of PBIS and family engagement.

It is important to keep in mind that there is an extensive overlap among these three core elements as most actions can be described as fitting within systems, data, *or* practices. This further demonstrates that it is the interplay among these elements that creates strong PBIS. For example, a goal of increasing behavior-specific praise could lead to systems planning such as staff training and administrator support; a data-related target such as increasing classroom-based data collection to establish a starting point and monitor progress; or a practice-related effort if we consider the effects of the intervention on student behavior and need to train parents to use this strategy at home. Consideration and planning around these core elements may be beneficial for identifying specific strengths and gaps in order to assist with action planning. We intend for the sections below to serve as a blueprint for conceptualizing PBIS and family-school partnership at any early childhood setting, which can be used to create, revise, or preserve PBIS systems, data, and practices related to family engagement.

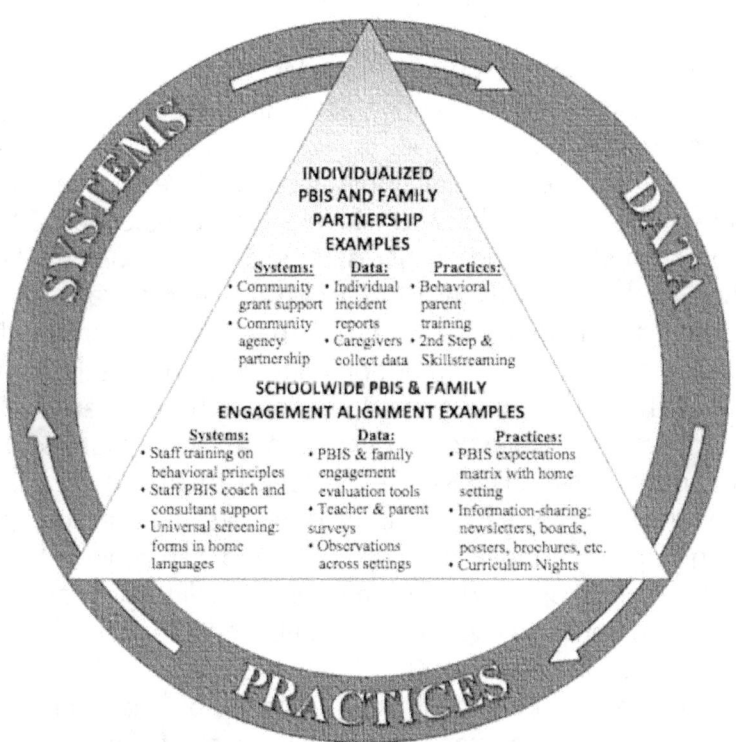

Figure 1. Examples of potential areas of alignment for PBIS and family engagement efforts within systems, data, and practices at an early childhood level.

Context

This case study is focused on the integration of family partnership efforts within a multi-tiered framework of behavioral support at one integrated public preschool in Agawam, Massachusetts that is serving children from age 3 to 5. District-level permission was granted to identify this setting to disseminate their efforts. During the 2017–2018 school year, approximately 160 students were enrolled at the Early Childhood Center (ECC) with 61% of students identified as having high needs (i.e., had a diagnosed disability, met criteria for being economically disadvantaged, or had a first language other than English; Massachusetts Department of Elementary and [MA DESE], 2018). The ECC is physically located across two different sites with one center including five classrooms, and another two classrooms located within a nearby elementary school.

Each classroom has up to 15 students, with seven identified special education students and eight tuition-based peers, with one licensed teacher and two paraprofessionals. Six of seven teachers have a master's degree and more than 15 years of teaching experience. This center is located within a suburban school district that began implementing PBIS district-wide in 2008. PBIS was extended to the ECC two years later due to the director's efforts toward district consistency and to ensure that students were familiar with a PBIS approach before transitioning to elementary school. The director of the ECC (fourth author) worked with an external PBIS consultant to plan professional development and advanced key components of universal PBIS (i.e., expectations, matrix, lesson plans, timeline for roll-out). The ECC, under the leadership of this director, has been implementing PBIS for 8 years and has achieved total implementation of up to 91% on the Tiered Fidelity Inventory (TFI, a tool that is commonly used to assess PBIS implementation across three tiers; Algozzine et al., 2014).

There are unique challenges related to implementation in this setting, with a primary barrier being lack of mental health staff (i.e., school psychologist, behavior analyst, school counselor) consistently assigned to the building. Additionally, implementation of program-wide expectations, teaching strategies, and acknowledgement systems across two different sites proves to be challenging. Strengths of the program include a high teacher-to-student ratio with experienced teaching staff who are well-trained in classroom management. Additionally, family engagement is central to the way of work at the ECC and there are many opportunities for ECC staff to interact with families. For example, the director has implemented programs such as Strengthening Families (www.strengtheningfamiliesprogram.org) and family Curriculum Nights to partner effectively with families of all students attending the ECC. In 2015, the ECC partnered with a local university to support their PBIS implementation efforts, as no technical assistance had been provided for several years. This partnership includes ongoing consultation from a PBIS consultant (first author), and the assignment of a School Psychology doctoral student to the ECC (second and third authors) to provide on-site technical assistance related to PBIS. This partnership led to targeted work to integrate and align strong PBIS and family-school partnership practices as well as increased attention to staff support and data-based decision making. The following sections describe examples of this effort to align strong existing practices within one ECC as well as components that were developed as a result of identified gaps or areas of need.

Family Engagement within the Key Elements of PBIS Systems

The PBIS framework emphasizes supporting student behavior to ensure success. However, the underlying behavioral principles equally apply to adults, and thus it is crucial for PBIS leaders to support staff behavior first (along the lines of putting one's own oxygen mask on first in case of an emergency before helping others). Systems within PBIS refer to organizational and structural supports that allow school staff to effectively and efficiently implement evidence-based interventions and serve as the foundation upon which data and practices can be built (Weist et al., 2017). Examples of systems in PBIS are team-based leadership, school-wide social-emotional and behavioral screening, and ongoing professional development for staff. Family engagement practices can be easily incorporated within PBIS systems such as having parental input in PBIS planning or professional development opportunities focused on culturally responsive communication practices.

At the universal level, all staff at the ECC receive ongoing professional development and training regarding behavioral practices, social-emotional development, and family engagement. This ensures that all teachers can implement sound techniques to support student outcomes in their classrooms. The skills and knowledge gained by staff through professional development benefit families as well through information-sharing. In addition, the ECC director, who serves as the PBIS coach, has systems in place to provide on-going support to all staff members via faculty meetings and individual consultation. Support focuses on improving school- and class-wide behavior prevention and management strategies as well as ways to collaborate with families. There are both formal and informal opportunities for teachers and family members to talk with PBIS leaders, which allows for open dialogue. To supplement professional learning, staff have also received handouts on topics such as family engagement and universal behavioral management techniques. Although handouts in-and-of-themselves are a rather passive tool, receipt of these materials coupled with encouragement to discuss and ask questions serves to emphasize to teachers that their director/PBIS coach is ready to listen and provide support.

Universal screening, another example of the PBIS systems, allows schools to provide more targeted prevention and intervention services to students at risk for behavior problems. The ECC has worked hard in the past several years to establish a universal behavioral screening procedure using the Strengths and Difficulties Questionnaire (SDQ; available at www.sdqinfo.com), which is a brief behavioral questionnaire that probes emotional symptoms, conduct problems, hyperactivity/inattention, peer relationship problems, and prosocial behavior, and that has a parent and a teacher report form (Goodman, 1997). The forms and the scoring guidelines are currently free to download (fee-based online scoring is available). This tool has a parent-friendly design (e.g., uses simple language, all items fit on one page) and is currently available in 86 languages. A PBIS brochure has been included with the distribution of the SDQ to parents at the beginning of the school year to introduce and/or remind families about PBIS and allow them to provide their input around PBIS programming and current communication methods (e.g., whether they are receiving communication sent through email). Use of the SDQ in families' home languages may help to engage all families, including those that may be harder to reach. One family not previously engaged with the ECC wrote a note to the director to let her know how much they appreciated receiving the form in their home language. In the fall of 2017, over 20% of the ECC families reported a home language other than English. The SDQ were distributed in 11 languages (SDQ forms were not available in two languages) with a response rate of over 70%. Ideally, the results of the universal screening should be used to drive more individualized interventions with families raising children who exhibit problem behaviors. For instance, the ECC plans to use the SDQ data for more individualized parent training recruitment (e.g., by specifically targeting families that report at-risk or elevated levels of the impact of the child behavior on family life, which in 2017 comprised 9% of families who completed the SDQ) and small group social skills training for the students (in 2017, 21% of children exhibited total difficulties in the at-risk or elevated range according to caregiver report).

For the past several years, at the individualized systems level of PBIS, the ECC teachers have had access to a doctoral-level consultant in order to problem-solve individual student behavioral challenges. These consultants have been emphasizing the importance of the ecological systems approach and providing families with a more active role in data collection and intervention planning to ensure continuity between home and school. PBIS consultants were able to expand one teacher's behavioral management repertoire by introducing a low-investment, family-focused intervention called "positive parent contact" (for more information, contact first author) where teachers share positive information about a student's behavior several times a week using simple scripts sent via a families' preferred communication method (in this example, written notes sent home). The teacher implemented the strategy with two families at the end of the school year and reported that she found the intervention to be rewarding and easy-to-implement. She was observed by the PBIS consultant to provide more behavior-specific praise to the target students throughout the school day and reported an immediate increase in reciprocal positive in-person communication from the caregivers (including a parent who in the past focused the conversation mostly on challenging behaviors). The parents were observed to show pride and excitement and praise their children when the notes were delivered at pick-up time. This is an example of how a brief individual consultation can empower teachers to partner with families in supporting student behavior.

At the ECC, an additional layer of support for the families comes from ongoing community collaboration. The ECC director has been involved with a Coordinated Family and Community Engagement grant, funded through the Massachusetts Department of Early Education and Care. The Outreach Coordinator for this grant is a parent of children in the district who gathers and provides input representative of parent and community perspectives to inform programming. Although the services provided by this grant are not limited to the ECC, ECC families are encouraged to take advantage of the free-of-charge activities, playgroups, social groups, and parent education opportunities available in their community. Parent workshops are organized around the Strengthening Families Protective Factors (www.cssp.org/young-children-their-families/strengtheningfamilies/about), which are aligned with the emphasis on prevention and relationships within PBIS, and parents are supported in their use of the Ages and Stages Questionnaire (available for purchase at www.agesandstages.com) to understand their child's development and ask informed questions of teachers and other service providers. Additionally, in response to an increase in the presentation of social/emotional/behavioral health concerns in young children, along with the desire to implement effective early intervention services, the district partnered with a community behavioral health organization to pilot a program to provide caregivers with increased information on, and access to, community support services. Potentially eligible families are identified through a home visit and biopsychosocial assessment, which includes developmental and family history. This information gathering is done collaboratively between the ECC and community agency staff. Families demonstrating needs are connected with community services ranging from food pantries and transportation through comprehensive inpatient, outpatient, or home-based behavioral health services. School staff who work with parents during the special education evaluation process were also trained in family partnership strategies and to provide information about the program to families. Parents, teachers, and clinicians have all reported high levels of satisfaction with this pilot program and therefore this will continue into the next school year.

Data

Data is an essential component of PBIS and is necessary for decision making. Data is a broad concept and is not limited to recordings of direct observations of behavior or environment over long periods of time in graph or table formats. Any information that can help PBIS teams identify current status, hypothesize problem or need for change, investigate effects of an intervention, or support decision-making is valuable. However, data collection can become a stumbling block. Data-related concerns were shown to comprise over 80% of requests for coaching during the first year of PBIS implementation (Scott & Martinek, 2006). It is important for PBIS teams to keep in mind that data are only a powerful tool if it is being actively used; otherwise, it can be viewed as a burden. One way to overcome staff reluctance is to start by (re)introducing teachers to simple strategies such as frequency counts and showing how these data guide intervention (Hershfeldt, Pell, Sechrest, Pas, & Bradshaw, 2012).

At the ECC, data are collected at the program, classroom, and student level; in groups and with individuals; by administrators, staff, and families. When it comes to family engagement, parental input has been sought to plan, evaluate, and enhance school and classroom practices. Last spring, the director sought input about universal practices through a family survey about 1) satisfaction with the level of information received about classroom activities, child development and behavior, and community events; 2) perspectives on the strengths of the ECC; and 3) whether their questions/concerns are addressed in a timely and effective manner. Caregivers reported high satisfaction with communication, particularly with weekly newsletters sent over email. Parents reported the ECC staff as the primary strength of the center along with the predictable structure and routine. This family input has been used to continuously improve upon universal family engagement practices. At the secondary and tertiary tiers, parents of students with challenging behaviors often serve as sources of information (e.g., via interviews and informal check-ins), provide data on home behavior or settings events for the teacher to be aware of (e.g., through home-school notes or in person), and take part in intervention planning (e.g., provide information on child preferences for reinforcement) to ensure buy-in and a cross-setting approach to addressing challenging behaviors.

At the universal level, PBIS teams have options of tools to assess current status and implementation fidelity, many of which have a family component where caregivers serve either as information sources, intervention agents, or decision-makers. At the ECC, the TFI (Algozzine et al., 2014; available at www.pbis.org) has been used over the past several years to guide PBIS planning, with scores ranging from 69% (2015) to 91% (2017) for overall implementation. TFI is a measure used to identify to what extent school staff are using core features of PBIS at each tier. This instrument can be used over time to gauge progress and identify areas of potential improvement. Family appears as either part of the item description or possible data source for 13 out of 45 items. Ratings on these specific items highlight that the ECC would benefit from having a caregiver as a member of their PBIS team to provide detailed input from the family perspective, and this is a targeted action step for the upcoming school year.

The PBIS coach at the ECC has used surveys and questionnaires to evaluate family engagement practices from the perspective of parents and teachers. For example, the Strengthening Families Self-Assessment Tool for Center-Based Early Care and Education Programs (available at www.cssp.org) asked teachers to respond to items related to the five Strengthening Families protective factors with moderately high ratings demonstrating that teachers focus on providing concrete support in times of need, build child social-emotional competence, and support families in their knowledge of parenting and child development. The Early Childhood Benchmarks of Quality survey (available at www.pbis.org) confirmed that focusing PBIS team efforts on enhancing family-school partnership is an important goal as every item on the "Family Involvement" subscale was rated as "partially in place" in the fall of 2017. In addition, last year, several teachers completed the Assessing Behavioral Support in Early Childhood Settings section of the Early Childhood Self-Assessment Survey (available at www.pbis.org) reporting that although family involvement in individual student behavior plans has been in place at the ECC, some classrooms might benefit from additional systems-level supports in their efforts to engage families. Finally, the Parent Contact Survey created to gauge teacher-parent communication practices (available from second author upon request) highlighted both staff strengths regarding family engagement (e.g., recognizing that each family has their own unique preferences regarding the mode of communication) and areas in need of improvement (e.g., there is a lot of variability in how frequently staff invite and encourage parents to participate in classroom activities). The survey data also show that contact between teachers and parents is most likely to happen in person (83% at arrival/dismissal and 67% during parent-teacher conferences) or over the phone (67%), although email (50%), class newsletters and websites (50%), home visits (17%), and notes (17%) are also frequently used. All staff agreed that family engagement is important for student success, citing "consistency across settings," "working together to support students," "creating more positive school experience," and "generalizing skills" as the main reasons. Other universal data sources related to family engagement have included school improvement plans, informal and formal observations throughout various school settings (e.g., hallways, parking lots), and data gathered with parents through the Coordinated Family and Community Engagement grant.

At the ECC, each teacher has developed their own methods to track and reinforce behavior among students in their classroom. When a student is noted to be exhibiting chronic or ongoing behavioral automatically challenges, the teacher and ECC director will initiate an incident reporting system developed using the district Google Drive account. Staff input data in a Google Form, which allows them to track behavior over time within a Google Sheet that can be shared with the problem-solving team (which often includes parents). The form was developed to model a referral form used within the PBIS School-Wide Information System (SWIS; www.pbisapps.org), although the ECC only used SWIS briefly during their initial PBIS implementation and found that it required modification of referral categories to fit the ECC needs.

At the individual level, students receiving interventions have ongoing data collection on their target behaviors prior to, during, and following the intervention. These data are frequently shared with the families when planning for or evaluating the effectiveness of the intervention. In addition, parental input is used extensively in individual behavioral plans at all stages of implementation. Families are integrally involved in function-based assessment processes for students with the most challenging behaviors, and family input is combined with data gathered at school to determine appropriate intervention strategies. When family members assist with intervention implementation (e.g., family activities are used as part of the reinforcement for appropriate behavior), behavioral interventions carry over to the home environment, creating continuity of care and enhancing generalization of skills taught.

Practices

Practices, or the research-based, scientifically-validated interventions and strategies used to support student behavior, are the most visible layer of PBIS. Those with limited experience with PBIS might assume that the practices are all that PBIS is. However, sound systems, such as professional training for staff members and dedicated intervention planning time, must be in place for practices to be truly effective. Furthermore, practices must be driven by data at all stages of implementation. When implemented with fidelity, PBIS practices increase the likelihood of student behavioral and academic success (Horner et al., 2009). Many PBIS practices already have or could be modified to have a family component and can strengthen family-school partnerships (Hemmeter et al., 2007; Weist et al., 2017).

Universal PBIS practices. Universal PBIS practices, for instance teaching school-wide behavioral expectations and specific praise to acknowledge prosocial behaviors, help establish and maintain safe, predictable, and positive school environments. At the ECC, the universal behavioral expectations (i.e., "Way to Bee at ECC: Be Safe, Be Ready, Be Kind") are displayed throughout the school, referred to throughout the day, and are developmentally appropriate. The school council, which includes parents and community members, provided input on these three ECC expectations when they were initially developed. Completing the TFI has highlighted a need to create structures to get continuous input on these expectations from families. All teachers have lesson books with PBIS-specific lessons and supportive materials to be taught during the first four weeks of school with practice sessions incorporated into circle time and large group activities across different school settings (e.g., classrooms, playground, hallway). These lessons are strategically revisited in December and March each year as a refresher and to support students who entered the program later in the year. After each lesson, the family is given a certificate showing the lesson that their child has been taught and how this lesson relates to "Way to Bee at ECC." These expectations are also communicated to parents during school visits via hallway displays, through the PBIS section of the parent handbook, weekly teacher newsletters and daily classroom board updates, and a PBIS-specific brochure distributed to all families at the beginning of the school year.

The PBIS brochure includes the ECC's behavioral expectations matrix with expectations defined for each school-based setting to serve as an example for families to help complete a blank home expectations section. Thus, families are encouraged to use similar language for behavioral expectations at home and in the community enhancing consistency across the school and home environment. The ECC also introduces and reinforces behavioral principles to families by sharing a monthly "Early Years" newsletter, published by Resources for Educators (www.rfeonline.com/parenting). These include information about parent involvement and methods to promote success for young children, such as positive discipline and character development. A "powerful interactions" board was implemented two years ago as a result of the ECC director's involvement in a course through the Federation for Children with Special Needs. This prominently displayed bulletin board includes photos of classroom interactions and activities with descriptions of the academic, social-emotional, and behavioral skills students are practicing. The goal is to give parents insight into their child's school day, reinforce the importance of positive relationships, and offer ideas about skills to reinforce at home.

School-wide family events, such as a Curriculum Night where families are familiarized with the educational classroom activities, provide an opportunity to introduce caregivers to PBIS. The ECC staff have been observed to frequently use "Way to Bee" language and specific praise for appropriate student behavior in front of families (e.g., "Great job being safe by using walking feet in the hallway, Kate!") during these events. In addition, the ECC staff use these program-wide events to introduce families to behavior management aids (e.g., visual schedules and cue cards), which can be implemented at home to improve challenging routines. In the past, parental feedback at such events has been collected informally. In the future, the program director plans to create a more formal system for capturing attendees' satisfaction data (e.g., anonymous exit poll or a brief survey) as well as general comments regarding quality and quantity of family engagement opportunities, which will assist PBIS team in decision-making.

Class-wide PBIS practices. At the classroom level, the staff at the ECC use many common PBIS strategies to prevent behavior problems, such as visual schedules, posters, cue cards, pre-corrections, modeling of appropriate behavior, and verbal praise. As the PBIS mascot for the ECC is a bumble bee, teachers use "bee parts" (e.g., wings, antennae, eyes) as a class-wide group-based reinforcement contingency, which is a variation of other visual group-based reinforcement systems such as token economies (Jolivette & Steed, 2010). Teachers provide "bee parts" as reinforcement for specific "Way to Bee at ECC" expectations. Teachers often communicate class progress towards building a whole bumble bee to families as an additional level of reinforcement for the students and provide a whole class reward (e.g., pajama day, special snack, video, extra time outdoors) once a whole "bee" is formed. Classroom teachers often send additional communication to families when a reward is earned and seek input and contributions from families related to future rewards.

Another classroom-level practice is the use of a social-emotional curriculum called the "Early Learning Second Step" (www.secondstep.org/early-learning-curriculum). This program introduces the young students to self-regulation and social-emotional skills via brief teacher-facilitated lessons focused on learning, empathy, emotional management, friendship skills, and problem solving. The ECC staff integrate the PBIS expectations within the lessons and communicate information regarding the skills learned to the families via newsletters, class boards, and face-to-face communication. Providing parents with matching home-based activities on the skills that are being taught supports adults in their use of common language.

For more intensive skill-building for students who are at-risk for or demonstrating challenging behaviors, the ECC is using the Skillstreaming for Early Childhood program (www.skillstreaming.com). This program consists of a four-part training approach that includes modeling, role-playing, performance feedback, and skill generalization, and focuses on basic prosocial skills that are essential for early learning success. Skill areas include beginning social skills, school-related skills, friendship-making skills, how to deal with feelings, alternatives to aggression, and dealing with stress. The ECC staff share the summary of each lesson with caregivers and encourage them to reinforce the skill use at home and in the community. The program package contains materials and activities for the families to expand the intervention across settings. The ECC has prioritized curricula and resources that include materials to aid communication with families and enhance feasibility for teachers.

Individual PBIS practices. Family-school partnership is often most explicitly considered at the individual level with parent involvement required during the special education processes. Students who receive most intensive interventions typically require more attention and resources from both schools and families, thus communication and collaboration between home and school becomes essential and is often extremely beneficial for struggling students. At the ECC, home visits prior to enrollment are a perfect opportunity to set the tone for the home-school partnership and familiarize parents with the basics of PBIS. Home visits are conducted for ECC students transitioning from early intervention programs to special education in the public-school system. Home visits are scheduled regularly for families with the most significant needs to build the home-school relationship, offer support, and conduct brief parent training. Other examples of home-school collaboration practices to address and prevent challenging behavior are communication logs, home-school notebooks, individualized check-in check-out programs, individualized reinforcement systems (often with parent component for tangibles or adult attention), and parent input and collaboration around functional behavioral assessments and development and utilization of individualized function-based behavior support plans.

Furthermore, behavioral parent education naturally connects the realms of PBIS and family partnership and can be used school-wide or at a student level. At the universal level, the ECC encourages caregivers to attend "Parent Café" meetings funded by the Coordinated Family and Community Engagement grant. These events, which are free of charge and offer food and childcare, provide caregivers with an opportunity for casual discussions on important parenting topics (e.g., social-emotional learning, child development, and school transitions), to learn from each other, and to form supportive relationships with other families. In addition, parenting skill workshops were introduced during the last school year as an additional layer of behavioral support for caregivers. Parents who were able to attend reported that they found the information and materials helpful and that they planned to apply the strategies they learned at home. However, low turnout suggested that more targeted and effective recruitment is needed to ensure that those families who will benefit from the training the most are able to attend. In the future, a recently developed individual self-paced e-training called "Practiced Routines" (https://practicedroutines.com) will also be offered to the ECC families who are interested in gaining the skills to continue delivering behavioral intervention at home.

Finally, one of the most powerful ways to engage families and help students build strong social-emotional and behavioral skills is to establish and maintain a positive and welcoming school atmosphere (Weist et al., 2017). Supportive environments and nurturing relationships serve as a critical foundation for success in early childhood settings (Fox et al., 2003). It is especially important at the early-childhood level to demonstrate that all school staff are willing and eager to work collaboratively with families, as this may be a caregiver's first contact with the educational system since their own schooling and will likely set the tone for future school-related experiences (Weist et al., 2017). A central mission of all staff at the ECC is to ensure that families perceive them to be invested in each student's success and know that the school and home contexts share the goal of developing happy and healthy children. The ECC director is skilled in finding opportunities to show families that school staff are always ready to listen and assist. She can be found at the entrance of the school daily at drop-off and pick-up, greeting families by name and following up on previous conversations. These informal interactions can also serve to reinforce basic PBIS principles for families as is evidenced in the example below. It is important for school staff to know families, greet them individually when possible, and communicate respect and appreciation. This serves to create a welcoming and supportive environment in which families view the school as a partner in their child rearing. Without this foundation, it is difficult to achieve coordinated multi-tiered family engagement efforts.

Using Core Elements to Guide Planning for Partnership

Although it is typical to plan and evaluate PBIS via the tiers of implementation, this may lead teams to overlook important elements and focus only on practices to support students. At the ECC, problem-solving conversations were organized around the core

PBIS elements of systems, data, and practices to encourage strategic planning for how to support staff, students, and positive outcomes at the individual, classroom, and program level. When we shifted away from a focus on tiers toward these elements of PBIS, we found greater success in partnership efforts. We encourage other ECCs to organize planning and implementation in this way, and we provide an example below to illustrate how these elements were applied to address one specific challenge related to family-school partnership at the ECC.

Within PBIS we often focus on specific routines and settings. Parking lots are one often overlooked setting that represents an intercross between family, school, and community. The ECC parking lot could have been considered a safety hazard in the past; however, the traffic pattern was re-configured and sidewalks installed after advocacy from the ECC director [systems]. Although the parking lot is explicitly listed as one of the settings on the ECC PBIS matrix [practices], concerns were brought to the attention of the director. Several formal observations were conducted during the fall and winter of last year to collect data on the frequency of following the "be safe" expectation. At that time, data showed 100% compliance with the expectations [data] and the team decided to continue monitoring the situation. An increase in unsafe parking lot behaviors observed by staff and parents in the spring [data] instigated a discussion, which led the ECC director to implement additional preventative strategies. These practices included assigning staff to directly monitor arrival/dismissal, praising and rewarding students for following expectations, safety discussions with specific families who were observed not following the expectations, and contacting the Department of Public Works to install crosswalk signage [practices]. These small changes led to immediate improvements. Data indicated that the issue was intermittent and several potential explanations were considered: 1) warmer weather and a conclusion of the new playground construction made it more likely that families would stay outside after pick-up; and 2) due to the nature of the

ECC enrollment (date of birth rather than start of the academic year), new families may be less familiar with the expectations [systems, data]. At the universal level, both hypotheses suggested the need for strategic re-teaching of the safe behaviors to students and caregivers at multiple points throughout the year via direct in-class lessons, parent newsletters, and increased reinforcement for following "be safe" expectations in the parking lot [systems, practices]. At the individual level, reinforcement systems may be necessary for students and families who do not respond to the school-wide interventions [practices]. Training parents in the use of behavior-management strategies may also be appropriate [practices]. Going forward, data (both formal observations and informal reports) will be used to monitor the effects of these interventions, amplifying, maintaining, or fading as needed [data]. With the goal of increasing safe parking lot behavior among ECC families, we used a problem-solving approach that relied on strong *systems* and *data* to create more targeted intervention plans within existing *practices*.

Summary

Although research supports the implementation of PBIS in home and school settings for young children, little attention has been given to aligning family-school partnership and PBIS in preschool settings. This may be particularly important given the benefits of early intervention for young children and may set the stage for ongoing family engagement to benefit students, families, and teachers. Data, systems, and practices are core features of a PBIS framework, and these elements can serve as a skeleton upon which strategies and resources can be developed to encourage family-school partnership that fit within the unique context of each ECC. As is demonstrated throughout the case example, it is imperative to proactively plan and strategize how to best engage families in behavioral and social-emotional programming. A multi-tiered model of PBIS serves as a natural framework to engage all families in partnering with schools to promote their child's success.

References

Algozzine, B., Barrett, S., Eber, L., George, H., Horner, R., Lewis, T., ... Sugai, G. (2014). *School-wide PBIS tiered fidelity inventory*. OSEP Technical Assistance Center on Positive Behavioral Interventions and Supports. Retrieved from www.pbis.org

Allen, R., & Steed, E. A. (2016). Culturally responsive pyramid model practices: Program-wide positive behavior support for young children. *Topics in Early Childhood Special Education, 36*(3), 165–175. Retrieved from https://doi.org/10.1177/0271121416651164

Bronfenbrenner, U. (1977). Toward an experimental ecology of human development. *American Psychologist, 32*, 513–531.

Dunlap, G., Ester, T., Langhans, S., & Fox, L. (2006). Functional communication training with toddlers in home environments. *Journal of Early Intervention, 28*(2), 81–96. Retrieved from https://doi.org/10.1177/105381510602800201

Epstein, R., Fonnesbeck, C., Williamson, E., Kuhn, T., Lindegren, M. L., Rizzone, K., ... Wright, G. W. (2015). *Psychosocial and pharmacologic interventions for disruptive behavior in children and adolescents*. Rockville, MD: Agency for Healthcare Research and Quality.

Fan, X. & Chen, M. (2001). Parent involvement and student's academic achievement: A meta-analysis. *Educational Psychology Review, 13*, 1–22. Retrieved from https://doi.org/10.1023/A:1009048817385

Fox, L., Dunlap, G., Hemmeter, M. L., Joseph, G. E., & Strain, P. S. (2003). The teaching pyramid: A model for supporting social competence and preventing challenging behavior in young children. *Young Children, 58*(4), 48–52.

Garbacz, S. A., Sheridan, S. M., Koziol, N. A., Kwon, K, & Holmes, S. R. (2015). Congruence in parent-teacher communication: Implications for the efficacy of CBC for students with behavioral concerns. *School Psychology Review, 44*, 150–168. Retrieved from https://doi.org/10.17105/spr-14-0035.1

Goodman, R. (1997). The Strengths and Difficulties Questionnaire: A research note. *Journal of Child Psychology and Psychiatry, 38*(5), 581–586.

Hemmeter, M. L., Fox, L., Jack, S., & Broyles, L. (2007). A program-wide model of positive behavior support in early childhood settings. *Journal of Early Intervention, 29*(4), 337–355. Retrieved from https://doi.org/10.1177/105381510702900405

Hershfeldt, P. A., Pell, K., Sechrest, R., Pas, E. T., & Bradshaw, C. P. (2012). Lessons learned coaching teachers in behavior management: The PBIS plus coaching model. *Journal of Educational and Psychological Consultation, 22*(4), 280–299. Retrieved from https://doi.org/10.1080/10474412.2012.731293

Holtz, C. A., Fox, R. A., & Meurer, J. R. (2015). Incidence of behavior problems in toddlers and preschool children from families living in poverty. *The Journal of Psychology,*

149(2), 161–174. Retrieved from https://doi.org/10.1080/00223980.2013.853020

Horner, R. H., Sugai, G., & Anderson, C. M. (2010). Examining the evidence base for school-wide positive behavior support. *Focus on Exceptional Children, 42*(8), 1–14.

Horner, R. H., Sugai, G., Smolkowski, K., Eber, L., Nakasato, J., Todd, A. W., & Esperanza, J. (2009). A randomized, wait-list controlled effectiveness trial assessing school-wide positive behavior support in elementary schools. *Journal of Positive Behavior Interventions, 11*(3), 133–144. Retrieved from https://doi.org/10.1177/1098300709332067

Jolivette, K., & Steed, E. A. (2010). Classroom management strategies for young children with challenging behavior within early childhood settings. *NHSA Dialog, 13*(3), 198–213. Retrieved from https://doi.org/10.1080/15240754.2010.492358

Jolstead, K. A., Caldarella, P., Hansen, B., Korth, B. B., Williams, L., & Kamps, D. (2017). Implementing positive behavior support in preschools: An exploratory study of CW-FIT Tier 1. *Journal of Positive Behavior Interventions, 19*(1), 48–60. Retrieved from https://doi.org/10.1177/1098300716653226

Lucyshyn, J. M., Fossett, B., Bakeman, R., Cheremshynski, C., Miller, L., Lohrmann, S., …Irvin, L. K. (2015). Transforming parent-child interaction in family routines: Longitudinal analysis with families of children with developmental disabilities. *Journal of Child and Family Studies, 24*(12), 3526–3541. Retrieved from https://doi.org/10.1007/s10826-015-0154-2

Massachusetts Department of Elementary and Secondary Education. (2018). *School and district profiles.* Retrieved from http://profiles.doe.mass.edu

McCabe, L. A., & Frede, E. C. (2007). *Challenging behaviors and the role of preschool education.* Retrieved from http://nieer.org/wp-content/uploads/2016/08/20-1.pdf

McCart, A., Lee, J., Frey, A. J., Wolf, N., Choi, J. H., & Haynes, H. (2010). Response to intervention in early childhood centers: A multi-tiered approach promoting family engagement. *Early Childhood Services, 4*(2), 87–104. Retrieved from https://www.researchgate.net/publication/234026975

Phaneuf, L., & McIntyre, L. L. (2011). The application of a three-tier model of intervention to parent training. *Journal of Positive Behavior Interventions, 13*(4), 198–207. Retrieved from https://doi.org/10.1177/ 1098300711405337

Reinke, W. M., Splett, J. D., Robeson, E. N., & Offutt, C. A. (2009). Combining school and family interventions for the prevention and early intervention of disruptive behavior problems in children: A public health perspective. *Psychology in the Schools, 46*(1), 33–43.

Scott, T. M., & Martinek, G. (2006). Coaching positive behavior support in school settings: Tactics and data-based decision making. *Journal of Positive Behavior Interventions, 8*(3), 165-173. Retrieved from https://doi.org/10.1177/10983007060080030501

Stanton-Chapman, T. L., Walker, V. L., Voorhees, M. D., & Snell, M. E. (2016). The evaluation of a three-tier model of positive behavior interventions and supports for preschoolers in Head Start. *Remedial and Special Education, 37*(6), 333–344. Retrieved from https://doi.org/10.1177/0741932516629650

Steed, E. A., Pomerleau, T., Muscott, H., & Rohde, L. (2013). Program-wide positive behavioral interventions and supports in rural preschools. *Rural Special Education Quarterly, 32*(1), 38–46. Retrieved from https://doi.org/10.1177/875687051303200106

Sugai, G., & Horner, R.H. (2002). The evolution of discipline practices: School-wide positive behavior supports. *Child & Family Behavior Therapy, 24*(1–2), 23–50. Retrieved from https://doi.org/10.1300/J019v24n01_03

Weist, M. D., Garbacz, S. A., Lane, K. L., & Kincaid, D. (2017). *Aligning and integrating family engagement in Positive Behavioral Interventions and Supports (PBIS): Concepts and strategies for families and schools in key contexts.* Center for Positive Behavioral Interventions and Supports. Eugene, OR: University of Oregon Press.

Implementing Family Education Programs in Preschool Settings
Stacy L. Bender and Sarah Fefer

Abstract

Family involvement in preschool has been linked to positive outcomes for young children. Family education programs, which refers to training or intervention that helps parents acquire skills and strategies needed to build a healthy family and successful children (Halle et al., 2015), are particularly promising. Despite the promise, there is little available research related to implementation of family education in school settings. Using an implementation science framework (Bertram, Blase, & Fixsen, 2015), this paper introduces key considerations for the exploration, installation, implementation, and evaluation stages of initiating family education programs in preschool. The authors also discuss their experiences, strategies, and ways to adapt parent education programs. Thus, the purpose of this paper is to provide a guide and descriptions of factors that practitioners and researchers may consider when implementing family education programs for their parent populations.

Keywords: **parent education, family engagement, intervention implementation, preschool**

Family engagement is essential for the behavioral and academic success of preschool students (Marcon, 1999) and parent involvement in intervention implementation contributes to favorable outcomes for young children with disabilities (LeBel, Chafouleas, Britner, & Simonsen, 2012). Families also experience benefits from school involvement including improved communication with their children, improved support systems with other parents, and an increased understanding of school programs (Epstein & Sanders, 2002). Multiple family engagement models have been proposed with most including examples of home-based and school-based involvement activities (Hoover-Dempsey et al., 2005). Epstein and associates' (2009) model of parent involvement in school is one of the most prominent and describes six types of parent involvement including parenting, communicating, volunteering, learning at home, decision making, and collaborating with the community.

Family education, a specific practice that spans multiple involvement types, refers to training or intervention that helps families acquire skills and strategies needed to build a healthy family and raise successful children (Halle et al., 2015). This method of family engagement may be particularly promising as parents themselves are provided with direct support within the school building, partners with parents to meet their needs and ultimately allows for greater connection between the school and parents. This is unlike many other traditional family engagement efforts that often involve parents engaging only as supporters and observers (Warren, Hoong, Leung Rubin, & Sychitkokhong Uy, 2009) or parents providing their services to the school (e.g., Parent Teacher Associations, classroom volunteers). Family education can be used for families with identified challenges (tertiary intervention), families at-risk for developing challenges (secondary intervention), or to prevent the future onset of problems (universal prevention; e.g., Hoard & Shepard, 2005). Furthermore, while all parents may benefit from parent education programs, benefits may be greater for parents of children with disabilities. They may gain specific knowledge related to their child's disability, build parent-child relationship skills, as well as receive support from other parents experiencing similar challenges. Family education may improve parents' understanding of their child's educational context and enhance implementation of school-based interventions, thus leading to generalization of skills for children across settings (Weist, Garbacz, Lane, & Kincaid, 2017).

Family education programs are associated with a variety of positive outcomes for parents and children (Högström, Olofsson, Ozdemir, Enebrink, & Stattin, 2017; Kaminski, Valle, Filene, & Boyle, 2008). Some of the most well-documented outcomes include parental skill acquisition for the purpose of improving child outcomes (e.g., effective discipline strategies), improved parental knowledge or well-being (e.g., reduced stress, improved parental competence), improved parent-child relationships, and decreased child externalizing behavior (Buchanan-Pascall, Gray, Gordon, & Melvin, 2018; Kaminski et al., 2008). Family education can provide parents with a range of skills to support their children's needs in the home environment and is a cost-effective way to address the needs of multiple families at once.

Rationale for Family Education in Preschool

Pre-kindergarten is an optimal time to nurture family-school relationships (Powell, Son, File, & San Juan, 2010) and promote parent education. Supporting parents of young children allows them to develop a positive relationship with the school, understand the importance of their role in their child's education, and improve their knowledge and skills in working with school personnel in supporting their child's learning throughout their education. Parent education is also a key component of a comprehensive program to enhance family-engagement practices in early childhood settings (McCart et al., 2010). For preschool students with disabilities, it is even more imperative for schools to offer parent education given that intervention has an increased likelihood of altering a child's trajectory if provided early. Parent education is included as an essential component for successful intervention programs for children with disabilities such as autism spectrum disorder (ASD; National Research Council, 2001).

There are a variety of family education programs targeting social-emotional and behavioral development for preschool-age students such as Preschool Basic Program within the Incredible Years series (Webster-Stratton, 2001) and the Triple P–Positive Parenting Program (Sanders, 2003), which have empirical support for their effectiveness. The *Compendium of Parenting Interventions* (National Center for Parent, Family, and Community Engagement, 2015) is also a helpful resource that describes parent education programs. Many of these can be used universally for all parents as well as for parents of children with disabilities.

Despite the positive and well-documented outcomes of family education, this approach is not commonplace in preschools (Raffaele Mendez, Ogg, Loker, & Fefer, 2013). As is the case with many other research-supported school practices, there are barriers to the implementation of family education, and it requires intensive advanced planning. Limited empirical research is available to examine implementation of family education in preschool settings and less information is available to provide guidance to practitioners about how to feasibly implement these programs in preschools. Implementing parent education in school settings may have a broader reach than those implemented in clinic settings (Raffaele Mendez et al., 2013), and additional benefits such as enhanced family-school partnership.

Given the benefits of family education programs, and the importance of early efforts to prevent and remediate challenges and enhance family-school partnership, we focus this paper specifically around implementing family education within public preschool settings due to their responsibility to serve students with disabilities and their families. The purpose is to describe establishing, implementing, and evaluating family-education programs in preschools situated in school districts using an implementation science framework (Bertram et al., 2015; Halle et al. 2015). The implementation science framework was selected as this approach was developed to promote the application of research-supported approaches in applied settings. The authors' experiences with implementing various behavioral and mindfulness parent-education programs are described throughout to share ideas and further illustrate examples discussed. However, we do not focus on implementing specific family education programs in favor of providing a more flexible approach that can be used to integrate family education into any preschool setting and meet a variety of family and child needs.

Exploration

Develop partnerships. The exploration phase is a foundational step to designing or selecting a family education program that fits the needs and resources available in each school. Developing partnerships with preschools, if the relationship does not already exist, is essential. It is also helpful to gain partnerships with professionals with parent training knowledge/expertise or to find this expertise in district. One advantage to working with other professionals with parent-training expertise is receiving support on selecting or adapting family education programs. This person may also be appropriate to provide training for school personnel. If this person is from within the district, it will be more cost effective than contracting out with another agency or organization. Building relationships and partnering with family agencies in the community is also helpful as these organizations may already provide supports to preschool families and benefit from more connection with the school (at low or no cost to the district). If family education is a new initiative in the preschool or if there is hesitancy from staff or administration, it is important to understand their perspective for information on how to discuss the rationale for family education implementation and increase buy-in among stakeholders.

Another step required during this phase is considering school and district context, a realistic timeline, and the cost it will take to develop, train, prepare, implement, evaluate, and see positive outcomes of the program. It is important to balance the needs of families and desired outcomes with the resources available. A point to be emphasized is that real or perceived limited resources should not halt plans to implement parent education especially if there is evidence of need among families. Consider seeking administrative and district support and pursuing resources through partnerships with local universities or community service agencies. For example, the second author works with a district that partnered with local agencies to offer free workshops to families. A wide variety of workshops were offered to meet the needs of their families including banks offering financial planning and local mental health agencies offering workshops related to specific disability areas. Some districts we have worked with sought grant funding to support parent education initiatives and supplemented the cost of training, intervention materials, and stipends for implementers.

Ongoing evaluation of cost effectiveness is also essential to implementation success. Facilitators should ensure that all aspects of program costs are being fully considered and utilized. In one scenario, the second author's implementation site hired childcare providers for sessions that occurred during the school day; however, there was only one younger sibling who needed supervision so costs were cut by having existing school staff spend time with the child rather than paying for childcare. Cost effectiveness is now included in many grant applications, which provides additional rationale to consider cost effectiveness.

Needs assessment. Conducting a needs assessment can guide the purpose of family education programming by providing an understanding of the specific areas that need to be addressed. Several areas of need may arise from a needs assessment; therefore, prioritizing is important. This can be carried out by asking parents and/or teachers to complete a survey to analyze the classroom, grade-level, school or district level data, or requesting ideas of topics from parents and teachers. This assessment provides an opportunity to inquire what content parents are most interested in learning about, when they are available to participate (i.e., day of week, time of day), and preferred modality of the program (e.g., in person, online).

A needs assessment can also be used to identify the population that will be targeted initially for this service. Data may suggest that certain parents would benefit from particularly targeted programming and preschools may want to target these families first in order to make implementation more feasible. In one preschool the first author worked with, parents reported interest in learning about parenting practices. Closer examination of the data suggested that many of the parents had children with a new classification of ASD. With this need, and the preschool principal's desire to keep implementation manageable, it was determined that these parents would receive support through parent education specifically related to ASD first, and then parent education was offered for all parents later in the year.

Another way to collect data is to implement screening for all students. Screening can be a quick and efficient way to examine behavioral, social-emotional, or academic needs of all preschool students. Teachers typically complete screening measures about students; however, including families in the screening process allows for a deeper understanding of student functioning. In a review of school-based behavioral screening informants, it was found that parents rarely serve as informants within the screening process (Hendricker, Bender, & Ouye, 2017). Therefore gathering data from parents may be especially important when the goal is to link screening data to parent education programs.

Selecting a program. The needs assessment will help guide implementers to determine the content, who to include, and modality of implementation of parent education programs. However, additional factors such as cost, time, and training are also important to consider. Halle and colleagues (2015) provide an outline of topics and questions that a team may discuss when selecting a program. These include 1) fit; 2) mission, leadership, and climate; 3) staff characteristics; 4) training needs; 5) coaching and supervision needs; 6) staff assessment; 7) internal resources for the new program; 8) community resources and partners; and 9) data and technology needs.

Two additional considerations for program selection are whether the program is evidence-based and whether it is culturally appropriate for the population with which it will be implemented. Helpful resources to begin searching for effective programs is the Institute of Education Science (IES) What Works Clearinghouse (WWC; https://ies.ed.gov/ncee/wwc), which reviews the research and provides effectiveness ratings on various parent education prevention and intervention programs, as well as many other interventions, programs, and practices in education. Another excellent resource is the *Compendium of Parenting Interventions* (National Center for Parent, Family, and Community Engagement, 2015). This describes parenting interventions, delivery format of the program, child and family outcomes, who the intervention targets, training requirements and qualifications of the implementer, and startup and ongoing costs. It also provides a comparison of evidence across parenting interventions.

Plan for evaluation. It is recommended that in this early stage, a plan for evaluation is developed. This is to ensure that the data collected before, during, and after implementation will be meaningful for the school/district as well as for families. Specific types of data are often needed in order to leverage future district support for these programs, seek external funding to maintain the programs, or to determine what may need to be changed to better meet the needs of families in this particular preschool setting. Questions to consider include what type of data will be helpful for the various stakeholders, who data will be collected from (e.g., families, teachers, administrators), what will these data tell us, and how will this improve our work with families and students? Input related to evaluation plans should be sought from parents, school staff, and others involved in implementation to best meet the needs of the school and ensure buy-in from all stakeholders.

Installation

Staff selection and training. Staff may be selected or choose to contribute for a variety of reasons, such as their professional roles and responsibilities in the school, or their interest and/or expertise in the area. Staff training should consist of learning about the intervention ideally by the developers of the program/intervention selected or by studying the manual (Halle et al., 2015).

While training from the developer may be ideal, this typically comes with a high cost. It may be more financially feasible to have staff study the manual and attend professional development meetings to learn about the intervention and implementation from a staff member, professional, or consultant/coach who has experience with the intervention. Staff implementing the intervention should understand the purpose and content of the intervention, along with important logistics. Allotting enough time for staff training is an important component of implementation success. Gaining the knowledge and learning the skills of the intervention will enhance implementation integrity. It is important to acknowledge that some school staff may require less training to be effective in the delivery of family education than others, and to plan training needs accordingly.

The distribution of responsibilities across staff members will vary by school and team. Discussing and assigning roles and tasks for each member will improve effectiveness and efficiency and reduce redundancy and confusion. In one scenario with the first author, who was serving as a facilitator from outside the district, there was miscommunication about who was going to be responsible for sending reminders for parent education sessions (i.e., time, date, location). The school engagement committee in the district organized the recruitment of families but assumed that the facilitator would reach out to parents to remind them of sessions. However, the facilitator assumed that the school engagement committee would take on this role. This example illustrates the importance of distributing responsibilities and expectations of staff and clarifying with other committees how the parent education team may share similar goals.

Along these lines, communication systems must be set up prior to implementation. A system of who will communicate, how communication will occur, and how frequently it will occur will help staff feel supported. This also serves as a mechanism to receive timely feedback on how the intervention is going and what needs to be adjusted. Communication is more effective when it is a two-way, rather than a one-way process (Halle et al., 2015). While in-person meetings are advantageous for certain purposes, they may not always be necessary or resource effective. Communicating via email, phone, or text may be preferred depending on the team. These methods of communication could be overwhelming if they occur too frequently or they may leave staff feeling unsupported if they occur too seldom. It is appropriate for a variety of different communication methods to be used depending on the need and preference of staff.

When the first author worked with two preschool administrators, they met in person at the beginning, middle, and end of the school year to discuss planning, progress, and evaluation. During the school year, it was agreed that the author would email the administrators every Tuesday (the day after weekly implementation) to give a brief update on the sessions. This email prompted administrators to ask questions or share reminders with the clinicians. The author met in person with clinicians for supervision weekly and was available via phone or text for the clinicians when they were implementing the programs each week. Developing systems that align communication frequency with the needs of implementers will help programs run smoothly.

Advertising and recruiting families. Advertising and recruiting families for parent education is a necessary and important step. When recruiting, particular attention should be paid not to discriminate or over-include families of certain characteristics, and to ensure that families who are hard to reach are recruited. A common and feasible way to recruit families is to ask teachers to share family education information with their students' families. Principals and other school staff that families have contact with are also helpful in spreading the word or referring particular families to the implementer. Another method of selecting and recruiting families is through the use of a screener. Families of students identified as at-risk through screening could be individually invited to participate. The second author has had success with a teacher nomination approach to identify parents. An administrator asked each teacher to nominate several families from their class who they perceived may benefit from a school-home partnership to resolve challenging behaviors. A team of teachers and administrators examined the list, prioritized based on other data sources (e.g., attendance, behavior incidents), and developed a plan to invite the identified families personally. Invitations came from teachers and were framed around partnership. Approximately 50% of the invited families completed the 7-week training each time this method was used within an urban low-income school serving students in preschool through second grade.

Khavjou, Turner, and Jones (2018) examined recruitment strategies and costs for low-income families' participation in a behavior-parent training program for children with disruptive behavior disorders. Strategies examined included a Facebook ad, events/presentations, grocery cart ads, a Facebook page, a research study listing, a mailer ad, a university mass e-mail, a research database, organization/agency, a bus ad, school flyers, flyers, and a Craigslist ad. Results indicated that the Craigslist ad yielded the most families and was also low cost for families, as was Facebook and email. While all of these methods may not appropriate for recruitment within one preschool, results suggest that a combination of approaches may be optimal. Implementers should consider how many methods they can feasibly utilize or what resources are already freely available to recruit families (Khavjou et al., 2018). Providing recruitment materials in the parents' home language is important, along with being up front in advertising materials about parents who are best suited for the specific family education offering (e.g., specific languages the program is offered in, specific diagnoses or behaviors targeted, etc.).

Another integral step is to determine logistics of session implementation. Considerations include time of day and location of sessions. Typically family education programs targeting K–12 families are held after school. For parents of preschoolers, there may be some additional flexibility. For example, if a preschool program is half day (i.e., AM or PM sessions), families may be available during the school day immediately after drop-off or pick-up times. Families may already be at the school and view attending family education sessions as convenient. However, this is not the case for all parents, as some may rely on the school bus to pick up and drop off their child, and many parents work during the school day. Therefore, it is important to assess convenient times for parents to attend parent education. Holding groups at different times throughout the school year and possibly during non-traditional times (e.g., early morning, weekends) may increase parent participation in family education.

Offering parent education at the preschool may be convenient since parents may be familiar with the school. One challenge that may arise is finding a space in the school building that is large enough and where sessions can be private and uninterrupted. For example, classrooms, designated family gathering rooms, or meeting rooms may be available depending on when sessions are held. The authors have held sessions in the nurse's office, a large motor room, the cafeteria, and the gymnasium. We have encountered double-booking of a room and unanticipated interruptions during sessions that occur during the school day; therefore, it is important to plan ahead to minimize disruptions. Students and/or personnel walking into the room, technology difficulties, fire drills, or announcements over the loud speaker may occur as they would during a typical school day.

Holding sessions at the school may not always be convenient or comfortable for all parents. Ideally sessions should be held in close proximity to where parents live, and public transportation should be available to minimize barriers. Bringing parent education to families such as to community centers, houses of worship/faith, and libraries may improve convenience and comfort level. The second author has provided parent education at a community center in a local affordable housing complex. Not only is this helpful from a logistical standpoint, but it may also strengthen the relationship between the school, the families, and communities the families reside in. This is especially important for culturally diverse families given that school personnel often do not match the social identities and demographics of the highest needs families.

Additional considerations when planning for sessions include whether the preschool can provide childcare, food, translation support (live or in advance to translate specific materials), transportation assistance, and incentives for attending/participating (e.g., Heinrichs, Bertram, Kuschel, & Hahlweg, 2005). Addressing these practical barriers, as well as psychological barriers (e.g., resistance, beliefs) with families in the early sessions improves engagement for the duration of the program (Ingoldsby, 2010).

Format

An advantage of family-education programs is that they can be implemented in multiple formats although the most common is a group format. Advantages for a group format include resource effectiveness in terms of time and the implementer. Parents' interactions and validation of one another, normalizing the experience of raising a child with a disability, and using one another as supports have also been found to be advantages (e.g., Gross, Belcher, Budhathoki, Ofonedu, & Uveges, 2018). Parents also report higher satisfaction with group-based parent training compared to individual-based parent training (Gross et al., 2018). Groups typically consist of a facilitator (with experience of the content being delivered) and a group of parents. There are several factors to consider when determining how many parents to include in a group, such as purpose of the group, feasibility, and convenience. In educational groups or groups that are delivering information which would be beneficial to share with all parents, a large number of parents in the group would be appropriate. For groups that have a focus on changing parenting skills, such as improving the delivery of positive reinforcement or teaching child-directed play skills, smaller groups of 4 to 8 parents are ideal. This allows the facilitator to teach parents the skills, opportunities for modeling, and practice and feedback within the group, which is consistent with many parent training programs. This level of training is difficult if the group is too large.

Web-based parent-training programs are a possible way to expand parent training intervention reach (McGoron, Hvizdos, Bocknek, Montgomery, & Ondersma, 2018). Studies using a 7-session internet-based parent-management training (Enebrink, Högström, Forster, & Ghaderi, 2012) and the 8-week Triple P online program (Sanders, Baker, & Turner, 2012) suggested promising results. Another released self-directed online program, Practiced Routines (https://practicedroutines.com/) was developed specifically for parents of young children experiencing behavioral challenges.

Implementation

Session implementation. Prior to the implementation of each session, facilitators should spend time preparing content, gathering materials (e.g., presentation, technology devices, videos), copying or creating materials needed for activities, and purchasing incentives if they are being provided. Examples of incentives include snacks or a meal at the session, reimbursement for travel, or a gift card to a local store. Attendance, participation, and homework completion are often incentivized in parent education programs. Resources for parents to take home to enhance generalization of content should also be prepared ahead of time and can include handouts or magnets summarizing the key points of the session, suggestions of how to use the strategies learned, and lists of resources for further information about the topic discussed (e.g., titles of books and magazine articles, links to websites, videos, and smartphone applications).

Facilitators must try and make a strong connection with all families that attend. Building a relationship with families is just as important if it is a one-time session or a 12-week program. The more parents feel connected and engaged, the more meaningful the sessions are for them. Facilitators with knowledge about families are able to provide more relevant examples and make content applicable. The authors have used intake forms to gather information about families and have also used ice breaker games into the beginning of family-education programs. We have also found that having two facilitators present can be helpful in providing translation support, talking with parents and answering questions they may have, helping to individualize content, or providing support for parents with lower reading abilities.

Retention. While recruiting families to participate in education programs is a significant feat, retaining parents or having them return week to week is an even bigger one. It is not uncommon for the number of parents attending weekly sessions to decline over time. In a review examining attrition for behavioral parent training, it was found that 26% of parents drop out before completing treatment (Chacko et al., 2016). Given this statistic, a good deal of research has focused on strategies to retain families. Communication with parents early and consistently allows the implementer to also address barriers for families early, which improves retention after implementation is underway (Chacko, Uderman, & Zwilling, 2013). This suggests the importance of seeking family input related to potential barriers during early planning stages. Additionally, the first session sets the stage for remaining sessions and content and delivery should be planned carefully. Facilitators should consider: Is the first session informative, attention-grabbing, and does it make parents feel like it is worth returning for? Did the implementer establish a relationship with the parents?

Other strategies can also occur *before* retention declines. For example, making contact with families after they sign up for the program but before the first session and calling or emailing parents to remind them of sessions each week can be helpful. This allows the implementer to remind parents when and where the program takes place, what they can expect in terms of content and format, answer any questions they might have, and establish a pattern of continuous contact each week. This contact can also serve as a way to assess barriers parents may have to attending sessions, and allows the facilitator to address these before parents even begin attending to improve retention (Ingoldsby, 2010). An alternative to the parent education facilitator can be designated to contact parents. For example, the second author created a "cultural ambassador" position in one of her grant-funded projects. The cultural ambassador is a bilingual parent in the school who helps with calling and texting families to remind them of sessions and follow-up to see why they missed sessions. This strategic position allows for reminders to be shared with families and informs facilitators of the barriers families may experience resulting in missed sessions. These calls may not be as well received by families if they came from the university-based facilitators. It is important to take actions to ensure that parents feel comfortable providing their input about potential program improvements.

Evaluation

Evaluation involves gathering information to inform the overall effectiveness of programs. There are two types of evaluations to plan and consider when implementing family education: 1) formative evaluation, which is ongoing and serves the purpose of development and continuous improvement to enhance program content or contextual fit; and 2) summative evaluation to determine whether the family education program achieved the outcomes intended. The formative evaluation includes previously mentioned considerations such as seeking input from and assessing resistance among stakeholders during the initial exploration phase, assessing and evaluating district resources and needs, or conducting a needs assessment to inform the selection of a specific family education approach. These initial aspects can also be considered usability testing (Halle et al., 2015), and should occur before program implementation.

Formative. It is important to be mindful when designing and implementing methods to collect ongoing feedback from families. Formative evaluation can enhance retention and improve contextual fit. This allows implementers to determine if the family-education approach was an appropriate selection for the population served by the preschool. Many evaluations of family education programs include an acceptability or a social-validity assessment at the end of the intervention (see Finn & Sladeczek, 2001 for a review of common social validity measures). The acceptability assessment often asks parents to provide input about their perceptions of the content and delivery of the family education sessions, the ease with which they were able to use the skills taught in their daily life, whether the intervention was successful in meeting their needs, and if they would recommend this intervention to other families.

The authors have seen a benefit to asking parents to provide input related to acceptability in an ongoing way rather than only at the end of the program. For example, the authors have used weekly feedback forms distributed either at the beginning or end of each session to ask parents to reflect on specific skills taught. Parents answer questions about the facilitators, the aspects of the last session that they found most helpful, their use of the skill of the week, whether the session content influenced their parenting practices, attitude, and daily interactions with their child, and whether they shared the content with others. Other questions included if the session met their needs, if they would recommend it to someone else, and if they were satisfied with the session. Open-ended questions asked parents what they liked and what they hope to hear more about next session. This allowed the facilitator to modify content accordingly to better meet family needs. While it could be difficult to address every suggestion from parents by the following session, ongoing feedback is valuable for the current participants and allows facilitators to consider modifications or adaptations for future sessions.

It is important to collect fidelity data during the implementation of the family-education program. Implementation fidelity refers to the extent to which the intervention is implemented as intended by a facilitator, which enhances intervention fidelity, or parents implementing the strategies learned in the parent education program with their children. This leads to positive behavior change among preschool-aged children and their parents (Barton & Fettig,

2013; Eames et al., 2009). Measuring this is essential to ensuring that facilitators are following evidence-based practices and enhances the likelihood that the program will achieve the outcomes targeted. Fidelity is often measured through direct observations of intervention delivery or through checklists completed by facilitators indicating which components of the program were implemented (Harn, Parisi, & Stoolmiller, 2013). For example, the first author found it helpful to include a co-facilitator during parent education sessions to complete integrity checklists and conduct structured observations of parent engagement behaviors during sessions. Fidelity should be measured frequently with data used to inform and improve future implementation. Lower fidelity may not always reflect poor implementation and may reflect facilitator adaptations made to enhance contextual fit. It is important to develop methods to track modifications and adaptations made.

Summative. Once the program is fully implemented and aligned with the context and needs of the preschool setting, evaluation efforts should include assessment of short and long-term outcomes among children and families as well as impact on the preschool or community as a whole. Summative evaluation efforts should be guided by the original purpose of implementation and very clear goals and objectives should be defined early in the program exploration and planning phases. For family education implemented in schools, it is likely that the primary goal will center around student outcomes. It is also important to consider parent and family outcomes and specific skills or information learned since parents are direct recipients of family education. This may involve measuring long-term changes in the preschool (e.g., trends in special education referrals or incident reports) or community setting (e.g., increased use of community-based family support resources) to understand the broader impact of implementation. There are many decision points related to outcome evaluation including what variables to measure, the specific tools or methods that should be used to gain information about those variables, as well as the overall purpose of the evaluation. It is important to determine what variables are most valued by all stakeholder groups and those who are most likely to reflect changes as a result of the intervention and align with program content. When possible, existing measures with established psychometric properties (i.e., reliability and validity) should be used, and existing research should be used to inform evaluation plans. Determining the most appropriate methods to capture change as a result of parent education can be challenging and may involve some trial and error. For example, the second author initially used a true/false test included within a specific parent training manual to measure growth in parents' knowledge of behavioral parenting skills. However, this measure did not demonstrate significant change after the intervention despite evidence from homework and in-session activities that parents were mastering the concepts presented. This led to the development of a measure using video vignettes, open ended questions, and a rubric-based scoring system to capture growth in parents' knowledge of behavioral parenting skills. The new tool required more time but it captured skills gained in a way that is aligned with program content more directly.

Teams should carefully plan around the logistics associated with evaluation. Action planning should consider who will collect the data, how data will be collected, as well as timelines for data collection, outcome evaluation, and data sharing. Use of existing data sources within the preschool setting should be prioritized as these methods require little time and effort from parents. This may include attendance data, incident reports, teacher records of participation in class activities, or any other data that is kept as part of school records.

We have also used observations, surveys, and interviews for formative and summative evaluation purposes. While this is valuable data, it can be challenging to collect information from participants. We have found that we achieve higher response rates and completion of measures when they are done in session versus independently. This provides an opportunity for facilitators to answer questions and support parents who may benefit from assistance in reading or responding to questionnaires. Measures should be provided in parents' preferred language whenever possible, or directly translated by a native speaker. Incentives may also be needed to encourage measure completion. The second author gives parents a raffle ticket for each questionnaire they complete with a winner drawn at the end of each session for a prize. This has been an efficient way to encourage parent completion of all evaluation components and is more cost effective than providing a specific incentive to each participant.

A combination of different methods and sources yields the most comprehensive information about program implementation and outcomes; however, evaluation efforts should not be burdensome to families or take away from the content of family education. Evaluation is an iterative process, and all information gathered should inform future planning and implementation and be shared with all stakeholders (Halle et al., 2015).

Sustainability

The implementation-science framework supports and is directly related to program sustainability. This approach recommends that implementation teams consider before, during, and after implementation how the program will be continued in order to reach more families. Questions to consider include: 1) how will fidelity of implementation be maintained over time? 2) how will funding be replenished and protected? and 3) how to expand expertise within the preschool setting to ensure that there is someone available to implement the program even if staffing changes or funding decreases? These questions should be considered on an ongoing basis and link directly to future action planning. Sustaining the support systems that are established during the exploration, installation, and implementation stages ensures that family education can occur on an ongoing basis.

Conclusion

Research has found that family education programs, a form of family engagement, promote positive outcomes found for children and their parents. However, this approach is still not commonplace in preschools given the barriers and intensive advanced planning it requires. To increase feasibility of parent education in schools, the authors applied the implementation science framework set forth by Bertram, Blase, and Fixsen (2015) and Halle and colleagues (2015) to describe how practitioners and researchers could explore, select, implement, and evaluate parent education programs within preschools.

The goal of our discussion of implementation of parent education is to make this approachable and feasible in preschool settings as well as balance implementation fidelity with acceptability and fit. We believe in selecting research-informed and evidence-based programs and adapting the programs to fit within the context of the particular preschool and population of parents, students, and staff. Halle and colleagues (2015) suggest that facilitators work directly with program developers to identify the essential program elements and ensure that only essential modifications to enhance fit within the specific population or setting are made. Ensuring that data are collected throughout implementation (i.e., before, during, and after) improves retention and parent participation given that immediate feedback from families can be used to make adaptations to better fit the needs of parents. There is evidence to suggest that modification of program components may enhance sustainability, and program modification or adaptation is very common in school-based applications of evidence-based practice. Therefore, interventions with built in adaptations and clear information about active ingredients may be best suited for implementation in schools (Harn et al., 2013). Our hope is that school professionals wanting to engage families in parent education will carefully select, adapt, and evaluate programs to ensure that parents and students receive the maximum benefit.

References

Barton, E. E., & Fettig, A. (2013). Parent-implemented interventions for young children with disabilities: A review of fidelity measures. *Journal of Early Intervention, 35,* 194–219. doi:10.1177/1053815113504625

Bertram, R. M., Blase, K. A., & Fixsen, D. L. (2015). Improving programs and outcomes: Implementation frameworks and organization change. *Research on Social Work Practice, 25,* 477–487. doi:10.1177/1049731514537687

Buchanan-Pascall, S., Gray, K. M., Gordon, M., & Melvin, G. A. (2018). Systematic review and meta-analysis of parent group interventions for primary school children aged 4–12 years with externalizing and/or internalizing problems. *Child Psychiatry & Human Development, 49,* 244–267. doi:10.1007/s10678-017-0745-9.

Chacko, A., Jensen, S. A., Lowry, L. S., Cornwell, M., Chimklis, A., Chan, E., … Pulgarin, B. (2016). Engagement in behavioral parent training: Review of the literature and implications for practice. *Clinical Child and Family Psychology Review, 19,* 204–215. doi:10.1007/s10567-016-0205-2

Chacko, A., Uderman, J. Z., & Zwilling, A. (2013). Lessons learned in enhancing behavioral parent training for high-risk families of youth with ADHD. *The ADHD Report, 21,* 6–11. doi:10.1521/adhd.2013.21.4.6

Eames, C., Daley, D., Hutchings, J., Whitaker, C. J., Jones, K., Hughes, J. C., & Bywater, T. (2009). Treatment fidelity as a predictor of behaviour change in parents attending group-based parent training. *Child: Care, Health and Development, 35*(5), 603–612. doi:10.1111/j.1365-2214.2009.00975.x

Enebrink, P., Högström, J., Forster, M., & Ghaderi, A. (2012). Internet-based parent management training: A randomized controlled study. *Behaviour Research and Therapy, 50,* 240–249. doi:10.1016/j.brat.2012.01.006

Epstein, J. L., & Sanders, M. G. (2002). Family, school, and community partnerships. In M. H. Bornstein (Ed.), *Handbook of parenting volume 5 practical issues in parenting* (2nd ed., pp. 407–437). Mahwah, NJ: Lawrence Erlbaum Associates.

Epstein, J. L., & Associates (2009). *School, family, and community partnerships: Your hand book for action* (3rd ed.). Thousand Oaks, CA: Corwin Press.

Finn, C. A., & Sladeczek, I. E. (2001). Assessing the social validity of behavioral interventions: A review of treatment acceptability measures. *School Psychology Quarterly, 16*(2), 176–206. doi:10.1521/scpq.16.2.176.18703

Gross, D., Belcher, H. M. E., Budhathoki, C., Ofonedu, M. E., & Uveges, M. K. (2018). Does parent training format affect treatment engagement? A randomized study of families at social risks. *Journal of Child and Family Studies, 27,* 1579–1593. doi:10.1007/s10826-017-0984-1

Halle, T., Paulsell, D., Daily, S., Douglass, A., Moodie, S., & Metz, A. (2015). *Implementing parenting interventions in early care and education settings: A guidebook for implementation (OPRE 2015-94).* Washington, DC: Office of Planning, Research and Evaluation, Administration for Children and Families, U.S. Department of Health and Human Services.

Harn, B., Parisi, D., & Stoolmiller, M. (2013). Balancing fidelity with flexibility and fit: What do we really know about fidelity of implementation in schools? *Exceptional Children, 79*(2), 181–193. doi:10.1177/001440291307900204

Heinrichs, N., Bertram, H., Kuschel, A., & Hahlweg, K. (2005). Parent recruitment and retention in universal prevention program for child behavior and emotional problems: Barriers to research and program participation. *Prevention Science, 6,* 275–286. doi:10.1007.s11121-005-0006-1

Hendricker, E., Bender, S. L., & Ouye, J. (2017). Family involvement in school-based behavioral screening: A review of six school psychology journals from 2004–2014. *Contemporary School Psychology, 22,* 344–354. doi:10.1007/s40688-017-0163-9

Hoard, D., & Shepard, K. N. (2005). Parent education as a parent-centered prevention: A review of school-related outcomes. *School Psychology Quarterly, 20,* 434–454. doi:10.1521/scpq.2005.20.4.434

Högström, J., Olofsson, V., Özdemir, M., Enebrink, P., & Stattin, H. (2017). Two-year findings from a national effectiveness trial: Effectiveness of behavioral and non-behavioral parenting programs. *Journal of Abnormal Child Psychology, 45*(3), 527–542. doi:10.1007/s10802-016-0178-0

Hoover-Dempsey, K. V., Walker, J. M., Sandler, H. M., Whetsel, D., Green, C. L., Wilkins, A. S., & Closson, K. (2005). Why do parents become involved? Research findings and implications. *The Elementary School Journal, 106*(2), 105–130. doi:10.1086/499194

Ingoldsby, E. M. (2010). Review of interventions to improve family engagement and retention in parent and child mental health programs. *Journal of Child and Family Studies, 19,* 629–645. doi:10.1007/s10826-009-9350-2

Kaminski, J. W., Valle, L. A., Filene, J. H., & Boyle, C. L. (2008). A meta-analytic review of components associated with parent training program effectiveness. *Journal of Abnormal Child Psychology, 26,* 567–89. doi:10.1007/s10802-007-9201-9

Khavjou, O. A., Turner, P., & Jones, D. J. (2018). Cost effectiveness of strategies for re cruiting low-income families for behavioral parent training. *Journal of Child and Family Studies, 27,* 1950–1956. doi:10.1007/s10826-017-0997-9

LeBel, T. J., Chafouleas, S. M., Britner, P. A., & Simonsen, B. (2012). Using a daily report card in an intervention package involving home-school communication to reduce disruptive behavior in preschoolers. *Journal of Positive Behavior Interventions, 15,* 103–112. doi:10.1177/1098300712440451

Marcon, R. A. (1999). Positive relationships between parent school involvement and public school inner-city preschoolers' development and academic performance. *School Psychology Review, 28*(3), 395. doi:10.1037/0022-0663.95.1.74

McCart, A., Lee, J., Frey, A. J., Wolf, N., Choi, J. H., Haynes, H. (2010). Response to intervention in early childhood centers: A multitiered approach to promoting family engagement. *Early Childhood Services, 4*(2), 87–104.

McGoron, L., Hvizdos, E., Bocknek, E. L., Montgomery, E., & Ondersma, S. J. (2018). Feasibility of internet-based parent training for low-income parents of young children. *Children and Youth Services Review, 84*, 198–205. doi: 10.1016/j.childyouth.2017.12.004

National Center for Parent, Family, and Community Engagement. (2015). *Compendium of parenting interventions*. Washington, DC: National Center on Parent, Family, and Community Engagement, Office of Head Start, U.S. Department of Health & Human Services. Retrieved from https://www.acf.hhs.gov/sites/default/files/ecd/compendium_of_parenting_interventions_911_508.pdf

National Research Council. (2001). *Educating children with autism. Committee on Educational Interventions for Children with Autism. Division of Behavioral and Social Sciences and Education*. Washington, DC: National Academy Press.

Powell, D. R., Son, S. H., File, N., & San Juan, R. R. (2010). Parent-school relationships and children's academic and social outcomes in public school pre-kindergarten. *Journal of School Psychology, 48*, 269–292. doi:10.1016/j.jsp.2010.03.002

Raffaele Mendez, L., Ogg, J., Loker, T., & Fefer, S. (2013). Including parents in the continuum of school-based mental health services: A review of intervention program research from 1995 to 2010. *Journal of Applied School Psychology, 29*, 1–36. doi:10.1080/15377903.2012.725580

Sanders, M. R. (2003). Triple P–Positive Parenting Program: A population based approach to promoting competent parenting. *Australian e-Journal for the Advancement of Mental Health, 2*, 127–143. doi:10.5172/jamh.2.3.127

Sanders, M. R., Baker, S., & Turner, K. M. T. (2012). A randomized controlled trial evaluating the efficacy of Triple P online with parents of children with early onset conduct problems. *Behaviour Research and Therapy, 50*, 675–684. doi:10.1016/j.brat.2012.07.004

Warren, M., Hoong, S., Leung Rubin, C., & Sychitkokhong Uy, P. (2009). Beyond the bake sale: A community-based relational approach to parent engagement in schools. *Teachers College Record, 111*, 2209–2254.

Webster-Stratton C. (2001). *The parents and children series: A comprehensive course*. Seattle, WA: The Incredible Years.

Weist, M. D., Garbacz, S. A., Lane, K. L., & Kincaid, D. (2017). *Aligning and integrating family engagement in Positive Behavioral Interventions and Supports (PBIS): Concepts and strategies for families and schools in key contexts*. Eugene, OR: University of Oregon Press.

Coaching Families to Promote Social Emotional Competence and Address Challenging Behaviors for Young Children with Disabilities

Angel Fettig, Erin E. Barton, and Hedda Meadan

Abstract

Challenging behaviors have been identified as a primary concern facing families with young children with disabilities, as challenging behaviors identified in the preschool years are predictive of later negative long-term outcomes. An emerging body of research supports family coaching or consultative approaches that focus on enhancing caregiver confidence and competence in implementing evidence-based practices. When caregivers are supported to maximize children's opportunities for learning, positive benefits for children and caregivers occur. Family coaching to address challenging behaviors might be particularly important in the early years to prevent worsening of the challenging behavior and mediate long-term impact. In this article, we describe evidence-informed family coaching practices that have emerged from the empirical research. Examples of each coaching strategy, approaches to challenging behaviors, and other family coaching considerations are discussed.

Keywords: challenging behaviors, early childhood special education, family coaching

Challenging behaviors have been identified as a primary concern facing families with young children with disabilities (Doubet & Ostrosky, 2015). The high prevalence of challenging behaviors is especially troubling given that challenging behaviors identified in the preschool years are predictive of later negative long-term outcomes (Poulou, 2015). Challenging behaviors negatively impact families ability to participate in home routines and community activities (Lucyshyn, Horner, Dunlap, Albin, & Ben, 2012). Caregivers of young children with persistent challenging behaviors face stressful demands (Baker et al., 2003), which negatively impact their quality of life (Joachim, Sanders, & Turner, 2010). The stress of persistent challenging behaviors impacts experiences across multiple settings and contexts including home, work, childcare, and interactions with extended family or friends (Doubet & Ostrosky, 2015). Conversely, social competence in children predicts later academic achievement, job retention, and relationship success (Jones, Greenberg, & Crowley, 2015).

Challenging behavior is defined as "any repeated pattern of behavior, or perception of behavior, that interferes with or is at risk of interfering with optimal learning or engagement in prosocial interactions with peers and adults" (Powell, Fixen, Dunlap, Smith, & Fox, 2007, p. 83). Such behaviors could be externalizing behaviors such as hitting, kicking, screaming, and self-injury; behaviors could also be internalizing and might present as social withdrawal, avoidance of activities, and unexplained crying. In 2017, the Division for Early Childhood (DEC), the professional organization that promotes policies and practices to support families of young children with disabilities, developed a position statement on challenging behaviors that emphasized the important role that family-focused practices play in addressing challenging behaviors. In this statement, DEC outlined several specific practices that promote social emotional competence and address challenging behavior such as respecting families, focusing on strengths, and being flexible and collaborative (2017). DEC also emphasized the importance of building supportive and reciprocal relationships with families that demonstrate value and respect for the caregiving role.

Relatedly, an emerging body of research offers evidence on the benefits of family coaching or consultative approaches that focus on supporting caregivers, particularly in caregiver-child interactions (Powell & Dunlap, 2010). These approaches maximize children's opportunities for learning by teaching caregivers to be responsive during typical daily routines and interactions with their children (McWilliam, 2010). When professionals support caregivers to be confident and competent in implementing evidence-based strategies, children's opportunities for learning increases dramatically. For example, they might go from a 1-hour-a-week session with the interventionist to daily, multiple-hour sessions with caregivers. Thus, supporting caregivers in enhancing their child's learning and development which is associated with positive benefits for both the children and caregivers (Dunst & Kassow, 2008) and might be particularly important in the early years to prevent worsening of the challenging behavior and to mediate long-term impact (Fettig & Barton, 2014).

What is Family Coaching?

In recent years, several family coaching practices have been identified (Barton & Fettig, 2013; Fettig & Barton, 2014; Powell & Dunlap, 2010). Family coaching is defined as a set of adult learning strategies in which the coach (i.e., intervention provider/professional) promotes the learners' (i.e., family/caregiver) ability to reflect on their actions and determine the effectiveness of the practice used and develop a plan for refinement and improvement for future situations (Rush & Shelden, 2011). Unlike consultation frameworks, which often focus on identifying the child's needs and suggesting strategies (Ruble, Dalrymple, & McGrew, 2010), these family coaching practices are based on principles of adult learning, which assert that adults learn when they are actively engaged; have multiple opportunities to practice in the immediate, relevant context; participate in self-reflection and assessment; and are taught using a variety of methods (Dunst & Trivette, 2012). Family coaching allows the professional to use practices based on these adult learning principles to focus on caregiver-child interactions within the typical environment and routines, and support caregivers' skills and sense of competency with their children (Rush & Shelden, 2011). Family coaching practices support the increased confidence and competence of caregivers and establish a collaborative commitment to implementing effective strategies to promote their children's development and learning (Allen & Huff, 2014).

The role of the coach is to work alongside caregivers to support the learning and uptake of the strategies that promote children's development. Professionals such as school psychologists, educators, early intervention providers, and behavior specialists can serve this role as they work to support families. In this paper, we describe 10 specific, evidence-informed family coaching practices that have emerged from the empirical research: 1) planning for coaching, 2) focus on daily routines and activities, 3) practice, 4) role play, 5) self-reflection, 6) feedback, 7) modeling, 8) video modeling, 9) collaborative problems solving and progress monitoring, and 10) using mobile technology to support implementation. We also offer specific practices that family coaching can target to support young children's social-emotional development and address challenging behaviors. Table 1 provides descriptions of each of these practices with specific examples. To illustrate the coaching strategies, let us consider this brief scenario.

> *It is time to head to preschool in the morning and James and Tyra are trying to get their 4-year old daughter Livvy who has Down Syndrome to put on her shoes and coat to get in the car. James is trying to get Livvy's shoes on while Livvy is sitting on the kitchen floor kicking and screaming. Meanwhile, Tyra is trying to calm the 2-month old crying baby and telling Livvy that she will lose her iPad time in the afternoon if she does not get her shoes on right away. After 5 minutes of verbal reminders to Livvy, Livvy eventually runs out of the room. Tyra and James looked at each other exhaustedly and proceed to put both kids in the car without shoes and coats. They decided that this daily morning chaos has got to stop and they need to seek some support to address Livvy's challenging behaviors. James and Tyra decided to meet with the behavior specialist at Livvy's school, Amy, to discuss the challenges at home during morning routines.*

Planning for coaching. All coaching processes must start with relationship building and joint planning to clarify the caregivers' priorities and outcomes (Hanft, Rush, & Shelden, 2004). Family coaching should always be intentionally *brief and focused*. The professional should focus on minor changes to what the family is already doing within daily routines. Planning also should include supporting the family in identifying goals and outcomes. Goals should be positively stated and driven by the family's priorities and concerns.

Focus on daily routines and activities. The professional should operationalize typical learning opportunities during daily routines in homes with the family's own materials. Identifying learning opportunities during daily routines allows caregivers to promote skill development throughout the day. The professional should plan to support families in using specific strategies that involve *minor changes* to what caregivers are already doing. For example, the professional can teach a caregiver to give brief transition warnings right before heading to school. The professional needs to adapt and match his/her practices to the needs of the family and focus on family participation in their child's development and learning.

Practice. Multiple and varied opportunities for practice should be provided as a critical component of family coaching. Professionals might enhance caregivers' motivation to practice by focusing on helping with routines that are not working well. Professionals should create multiple practice opportunities throughout the day before, during, and after home visits. During the visits, caregivers should have ample opportunities to practice specific strategies such that the professional can provide support and *performance-based feedback*.

Role play. Role play can be used to support caregivers in practicing new skills. In this strategy, adults take on different roles in the coaching sessions to practice implementing the specific instructional strategy during their daily routines and activities. When caregivers are reluctant to try something new, role play might be

Table 1
Family Coaching Practices and Considerations

Practice/ Consideration	Description	Example
Planning for coaching	The professional should clarify caregivers' goals and priorities and focus on supporting caregivers in using strategies that involve just minor changes to what the family is already doing.	Amy engaged Livvy's caregivers in conversations to understand goals and outcomes that are meaningful to them. Amy learned that both caregivers already used electronic schedules on their phones. Amy supported them in referring to the visual schedule along with the verbal prompts they were already using.
Focus on daily routines and activities	The professional should support the caregivers in implementing strategies to support child learning and development during daily routines.	Livvy's visual schedule outlined the exact components of the family's morning routines.
Practice	The professional should allow multiple and varied opportunities for caregivers to practice.	Amy, James, and Tyra collaboratively discussed opportunities to practice using the visual schedule. This included helping Livvy practice so that she could independently use the schedule.
Role play	The professional and caregivers could take on different roles and practice specific strategies to increase caregiver confidence and competency.	Amy used role play with James and Tyra to support them in responding to Livvy when she did not follow the routines. James and Tyra took turns adopting the role of Livvy and the adult and Amy verbally walked them through the procedures to use.

Family Coaching, continued

Self-reflection	The professional should support caregivers in engaging in regular self-reflection regarding progress and satisfaction with the intervention and family coaching process. The professional should model self-reflection and engage in regular self-reflection regarding the efficacy of their coaching practices.	Amy encouraged James and Tyra to reflect on their own satisfaction with the morning routine and Livvy's behaviors. She sent group texts to check in with them about every 3–4 days, which prompted James and Tyra's reflection and discussion of progress.
Performance-based feedback	The professional should give supportive and corrective performance based feedback (i.e., based on the caregivers use of the strategies). Supportive feedback is positively stated and tells the caregivers exactly what they are doing well. Corrective feedback should also be stated positively, but should support the caregiver in improving or increasing their use of specific strategies with their children.	Amy provided feedback based on her observations (which were limited) and the videos Tyra and James sent her. She often sent feedback via text based on the videos. The feedback highlighted exactly what they were doing well and strategies they might improve upon.
Modeling	The professional could demonstrate specific strategies with or without the child. This should be followed by multiple opportunities for the caregivers to practice using the strategy.	During home visits, Amy modeled how to point to the visual schedule and give verbal prompts to Livvy each morning.
Video modeling	Demonstration videos or self-videos could be used to illustrate and provide feedback on the caregivers use of specific strategies.	During home visits, Amy modeled how to point to the visual schedule and give verbal prompts to Livvy each morning.

Family Coaching, continued

Collaborative problem solving & progress monitoring	The professional and caregivers should collaborate to identify when problems or issues arise and brainstorm potential solutions. The professionals should avoid always have the answers. The professional and caregivers should also collaborate to identify goals and monitoring systems.	James and Tyra told Amy that Livvy had started resisting the afternoon routines as well. Amy worked with them to use similar strategies across routines. Amy also worked with James and Tyra to rate the quality of the morning and afternoon routines each day using the "Notes" section of their smart phones (which they already used often for reminders and notes). They reviewed this data at the end of each week.
Use mobile technology to support implementation	The professional should support the caregivers in identifying software applications to aide in notetaking, monitoring behavior, providing visual cues and warnings, as well as remote check-in in between visits.	Amy identified visual timers for James and Tyra to use for transition warnings. Amy, James and Tyra also agreed on sending daily reminders regarding use of strategies and checking in via video conferencing in between visits.

helpful for increasing their comfort and confidence. Once the caregiver increases his/her competence with the skill, s/he can practice with his/her child.

Self-reflection. Self-reflection should be a key part of a coaching process as it allows both the coach and caregivers to examine progress and adjust implementation strategies accordingly. This ongoing self-assessment practice supports the coach and the caregivers in building capacity and skill acquisition (Gilkerson, 2004). Professionals should model and support caregivers in engaging in regular *self-reflection* regarding their child's progress, their sense of competence, and their satisfaction with routines, their child's behaviors, or specific interventions. Together, professionals can then work with the caregivers to tailor implementation and strategies to maximize their child's learning. The professional should also engage in self-reflection to ensure they are a) considering the context for family's priorities and concerns; b) respecting the family's values, beliefs, and assumptions; c) effectively communicating with families particularly when there are disagreements or difficult conversations; and d) seeking support from peers or other experts.

Performance-based feedback. Performance-base feedback is one of the most widely used strategies in coaching practices (Maturana & Wood, 2012). Feedback provided by the coach should be based on direct observations of the caregiver, actions reported by the caregiver, or information shared by the caregiver. The feedback given should be designed to expand the caregivers' current level of understanding about a strategy they are using or to affirm the caregivers' thoughts or actions related to the intended outcome (Rush & Sheldon, 2011). When coaching caregivers, the feedback given should be supportive and corrective. Supportive feedback highlights the caregivers' strengths and is positively focused. Corrective feedback should support improvement, include specific examples, and is linked to child outcomes. Feedback should always be specific enough to tell the caregivers exactly what they did accurately and what they might change to yield better or more desirable outcomes for the target routine.

Modeling. Modeling is intentional and directly demonstrates specific instructional strategies during specific routines. This strategy can be delivered live or with demonstration videos for the caregivers to see how a specific strategy is implemented. For example, the professional might model how to use a visual schedule to cue the child for the next transition. Modeling should be brief and focused such that the caregiver has opportunities to practice.

Video modeling. Video modeling might be particularly feasible given the prevalence and ease of smart phones and tablets with video capability. Video modeling allows professionals to use video recordings to provide a specific visual model of the instructional practice of interest. The videos can be demonstration videos of other caregivers using the practice or the professional might record the child and caregiver interacting during a routine to give the caregiver feedback. The caregivers could review these video recordings when it is convenient. Videos also can be an excellent tool for supporting caregivers in engaging in *self-reflection* regarding routines or specific practices.

Collaborative problem-solving and progress-monitoring. Collaborative problem-solving should be used by the coach and caregivers to brainstorm possible solutions to existing concerns and questions. Collaborative problem-solving should focus on strengths of the families, emphasize not always having a solution, and ask the caregivers about what they have tried before and what has worked well in other situations. This should be linked directly to *progress monitoring* whereby the caregivers and professional have selected a method for collecting and reviewing data. The child's outcomes, caregiver competence, and caregiver satisfaction should be closely monitored.

Using mobile technology to support implementation. Mobile technologies offer a viable option for providing ongoing support to caregivers when professionals cannot be physically present (Meadan & Daczewitz, 2015; Meadan, Meyer, Snodgrass, & Halle, 2013). Mobile technologies can be widely accessible, cost-efficient, flexible, and promote high fidelity implementation (Baggett et al., 2010). The Pew Research Center reported that in 2017, 77% of the United States uses smartphones (Smith, 2017), thus highlighting the appeal of mobile applications. Text messaging has become nearly ubiquitous as a form of communication and has been effectively used in many areas of education and healthcare (Bigelow, Carta, & Lefever, 2008). Aside from easily accessible timer and visual schedule software applications, mobile technologies present a great way for professionals and families to check in and receive resources. For example, professionals might send daily or weekly reminders to caregivers to check in regarding child progress. Professionals also can connect the caregiver with other caregivers to establish social systems of support and additional opportunities for knowledge sharing.

What Practices Do You Teach?

Family coaching should focus on enhancing caregivers' responsivity and capacity to support their child's development and learning (Kong & Carta, 2013) and caregivers' use of naturalistic instructional strategies embedded throughout daily routines (Salisbury et al., 2017). The next sections outline specific practices that family coaching should focus on when working with caregivers. The practices are based on the Pyramid Model framework for promoting social emotional competence and addressing challenging behaviors in young children (Hemmeter, Ostrosky, & Fox, 2006; see Figure 1). The framework promotes the use of family-centered, culturally responsive practices and has been effective in homes (Duda, Clarke, Fox, & Dunlap, 2008).

Promote nurturing, responsive relationships and environments. Nurturing and responsive relationships and environments are critical to social emotional development. Nurturing relationships provide a secure base for when scary or unexpected events occur, which promotes social emotional competence. In fact, adult responsivity directly shapes the child's overall development. Dunst and Kassow (2008) found that caregivers who were contingent (i.e., responded to the child immediately) and explicit (i.e., they responded in ways that were related to what their child was doing, in ways their child could understand) had the highest likelihood of having infants with secure attachments. Professionals should support caregivers in being explicit and contingent responders. Further, caregiving environments should be designed to enhance relationships and learning. This can be done through coaching caregivers to provide predictable daily routines, engage in positive interactions throughout the day, and provide frequent positive attention particularly when children are engaging in appropriate behaviors.

Targeted instruction. Targeted social emotional supports are for families with children determined to be at-risk for social-emotional delays. These are specific strategies targeted for caregivers to help their children who might need more intentional teaching and practices to promote their development or to prevent concerns or delays. The goal for implementing targeted social emotional supports is to support caregivers in being intentional about teaching and promoting social-emotional development. Family coaching focuses on supporting caregivers in enhancing their children's social emotional development by intentionally using instruction (e.g., specific strategies for supporting communication, independence, social skills, and play) within daily activities and routines. For example, the professional might coach caregivers in using incidental teaching during mealtimes to support their child's communication skills. The professional might teach the caregiver to place preferred items out of reach, wait for the child to indicate interest in an item, and prompt appropriate communication prior to handing the child the requested item. Professionals also might teach caregivers to use a visual schedule during the bedtime routine to support their child's independence in complete tasks.

Addressing and preventing challenging behaviors. Some children will exhibit severe and persistent challenging behavior even when nurturing and responsive relationships are in place in high-quality environments. For example, children who have limited social skills or have learned that challenging behavior will result in meeting their needs may also use challenging behavior instead of language. The first step is to seek to understand why the child is using the challenging behavior or the purpose or function of the challenging behavior. The research on addressing challenging behaviors in young children overwhelmingly points to the use of function-based interventions to reduce and prevent challenging behaviors (Dunlap & Fox, 2011), while focusing on enhancing caregivers' capacity to meet the needs of their young children with disabilities (Duda et al., 2008; Fettig, Schultz, & Sreckovic, 2015). The primary assumption underlying function-based interventions is the understanding that the challenging behavior is serving a specific function for the children (e.g., gaining attention, escaping a demand, getting access to a tangible item or activity). Caregivers can implement function-based interventions that focuses on utilizing prevention strategies to reduce the likelihood that challenging behaviors would occur, teaching the child new skills to replace challenging behaviors, and respond to challenging behaviors in ways that minimize the challenging behavior's effectiveness. With ongoing coaching and supports from professionals, these interventions are likely to reduce children's challenging behaviors and increase their use of appropriate social behaviors.

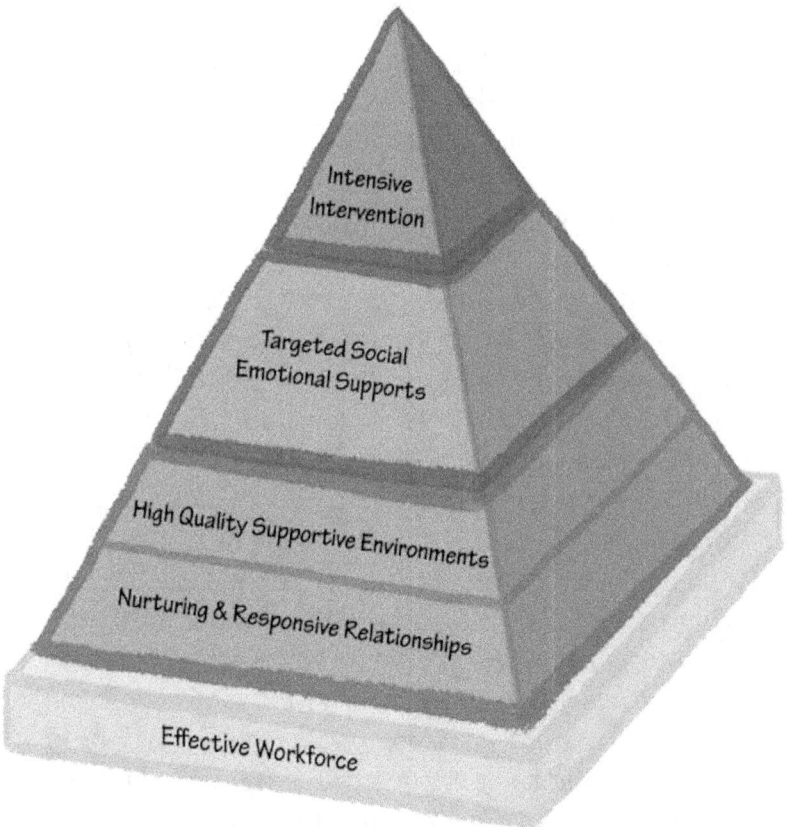

Figure 1. Pyramid Model Framework for Promoting Social-Emotional Competence and Addressing Challenging Behaviors in Young Children

Monitoring Family Coaching and Caregiver Implementation

Professionals must work with caregivers to make data-based decisions regarding the implementation of family coaching and caregiver instructional practices. Both professionals and caregivers could provide input regarding effectiveness of coaching. For example, caregivers could provide ratings on their relationship with the coaches, their confidence and competence in implementing the instructional practices to address challenging behaviors, and their satisfaction with the coaching process. Furthermore, caregivers' use of intentional teaching and child social emotional skills should be closely monitored and evaluated to make instructional adaptations. The most important aspect of data collection is that it is completed. This means the professional works with the caregivers to create "user-friendly" forms that are feasible and easy to use. This might include ratings scales, frequency counts, and behavioral checklists. The data collection system should eventually be used and interpreted without the coach's presence.

> James and Tyra met with the behavior specialist at Livvy's school, Amy, to discuss the challenges at home during morning routines. With the support of Amy, James and Tyra created a visual schedule for Livvy to follow during the morning routines similar to the one Livvy follows at school. During their coaching session, Amy role-played with James and Tyra regarding how the visual schedule might be implemented at home. She modeled how to use the visual schedule, how to provide frequent positive attention and praise to Livvy for appropriate behaviors, and how to avoid providing additional attention to Livvy for not complying with the morning routine. James and Tyra videotaped the implementation of the visual schedule at the home for a week. During their follow up meeting, Amy watched the videos with James and Tyra while they reflected on their implementation of the visual schedules and Livvy's improved behavior during

morning routines. Amy also worked with them to create a data-collection system to monitor their satisfaction with the morning routine. They discussed multiple options and decided to record their satisfaction with the routine on a note-taking app on their phones, which they already used often. Amy helped them set up a new note and share it with each other and with her so they could review progress together. Amy also sent follow-up texts every week with the same three questions to support their self-reflection about the routines: which strategies were successful, what was challenging, and what would you like to improve about the morning routine?

Other Coaching Considerations

Professionals working with families and caregivers must consider the individual family's diversity, cultural values, and parenting philosophy. Professionals must work towards cultural reciprocity and responsiveness through self-reflection of their own biases and believes around behavior and parent-child interaction. It is only with self-awareness that professionals are able to utilize culturally responsive practices to support families. Furthermore, when coaching families, professionals must understand individual family's preferences around communication strategies. Setting ground rules regarding frequency and mode of communications could enhance the coaching relationship and maximize parent and child outcomes. Additionally, written manuals on the target strategies could be useful for some families but should be developed to support family implementation of specific strategies and written such that all family members can utilize and understand. If professionals are coaching on the implementation of a behavior support plan for a child with severe and persistent challenging behaviors, this behavior support plan should always be provided in writing to caregivers. Professionals should also carefully monitor other interventions in which the family is engaged. Other interventions could enhance, impede, or impact the professional's efforts to support families in using evidence-based strategies to address challenging behaviors at home. This should be carefully monitored and collaboratively addressed. Lastly, coaching families to support the social emotional development and address the challenging behaviors of their children can be complex and emotional. When appropriate, professionals should direct families for additional services and support to ensure that family's overall wellbeing is achieved.

Conclusion

Challenging behaviors are a major impediment to family quality of life. The collective use of the practices outlined in this article ensures that professionals use evidence-informed adult-learning strategies including factual information, expert demonstration, opportunities for practice and rehearsal, and performance-based feedback. The research is clear that ongoing supports are needed to ensure that caregivers are confident and competent in supporting their child's development and thier social emotional competence in particular. Although the family coaching practices might be time intensive and unlikely to be available in home settings for all children with disabilities, the burgeoning use of internet and mobile technologies to support families is promising for reaching families who might not otherwise get home supports. Mobile applications might provide an innovative, effective option for delivering ongoing support to families. Policies and systems should be developed to ensure that caregivers of young children with challenging behaviors have access to evidence-based home supports. The practices outlined in this manuscript might make home-based supports and family coaching accessible, efficient, and effective for more families.

References

Allen, K., & Huff, N. L. (2014). Family coaching: An emerging family science field. *Family Relations, 63*, 569–582.

Baggett, K. M., Davis, B., Feil, E. G., Sheeber, L. L., Landry, S. H., Carta, J. J., & Leve, C. (2010). Technologies for expanding the reach of evidence-based interventions: Preliminary results for promoting social-emotional development in early childhood. *Topics in Early Childhood Special Education, 29*, 226–238.

Baker, B. L., McIntyre, L. L., Blacher, J., Crnic, K., Edelbrock, C., & Low, C. (2003). Preschool children with and without developmental delay: Behaviour problems and parenting stress over time. *Journal of Intellectual Disability Research, 47*, 217–230.

Barton, E. E., & Fettig, A. (2013). Parent-implemented interventions for young children with disabilities: A review of fidelity features. *Journal of Early Intervention, 35*, 194–219.

Bigelow, K. M., Carta, J. J., & Burke Lefever, J. (2008). Txt u ltr: Using cellular phone technology to enhance a parenting intervention for families at risk for neglect. *Child Maltreatment, 13*, 362–367.

Division for Early Childhood. (2017). *Position Statement on Challenging Behavior and Young Children.* Washington DC: Author.

Doubet, S. L., & Ostrosky, M. M. (2015). The impact of challenging behavior on families: I don't know what to do. *Topics in Early Childhood Special Education, 34*, 223–233.

Duda, M. A., Clarke, S., Fox, L., & Dunlap, G. (2008). Implementation of positive behavior support with a sibling set in a home environment. *Journal of Early Intervention, 30*, 213–236.

Dunlap, G., & Fox, L. (2011). Function-based interventions for children with challenging behavior. *Journal of Early Intervention, 33*, 333–343.

Dunst, C. J., & Kassow, D. (2008). Caregiver sensitivity, contingent social responsiveness, and secure infant attachment. *Journal of Early and Intensive Behavior Intervention, 5*, 40–56.

Dunst, C. J., & Trivette, C. M. (2012). Moderators of the effectiveness of adult learning method practices. *Journal of Social Sciences, 8*, 143–148.

Fettig, A., & Barton, E. E. (2014). Functional assessment-based parent intervention to reduce children's challenging behaviors: A literature review. *Topics in Early Childhood Special Education, 34*, 49–61.

Fettig, A., Schultz, T. R., & Sreckovic, M. A. (2015). Effects of coaching on the implementation of functional assessment–based parent intervention in reducing challenging behaviors. *Journal of Positive Behavior Interventions, 17*, 170–180.

Gilkerson, L. (2004). Reflective supervision in infant-family programs: Adding clinical process to non-clinical settings. *Infant Mental Health Journal, 25* (5), 424–439.

Hanft, B., Rush, D., & Shelden, M. (2004). *Coaching Families and Colleagues in Early Childhood.* Baltimore, MD: Paul H. Brookes Publishing Co., Inc.

Hemmeter, M. L., Ostrosky, M., & Fox, L. (2006). Social and emotional foundations for early learning: A conceptual model for intervention. *School Psychology Review, 35*, 583.

Joachim, S., Sanders, M., & Turner, K. (2010). Reducing preschoolers' disruptive behavior in public with a brief parent discussion group. *Child Psychiatry and Human Development, 41*, 47–60.

Jones, D. E., Greenberg, M., & Crowley, M. (2015). Early social-emotional functioning and public health: The relationship between kindergarten social competence and future wellness. *American Journal of Public Health, 105*, 2283–2290.

Kong, N. Y., & Carta, J. J. (2013). Responsive interaction interventions for children with or at risk for developmental delays. *Topics in Early Childhood Special Education, 33*, 4–17.

Lucyshyn, J. M., Horner, R. H., Dunlap, G., Albin, R. W., & Ben, K. R. (2002). Positive behavior support with families. In J. M. Lucyshyn, G. Dunlap, & R. W. Albin, (Eds.), *Families and positive behavior support: Addressing problem behavior in family contexts* (pp. 3–44). Baltimore: Paul H. Brookes.

Marturana, E. R., & Woods, J. J. (2012). Technology-supported performance-based feedback for early intervention home visiting. *Topics in Early Childhood Special Education, 32*(1), 14–23.

McWilliam, R. A. (2010). *Routines-based early intervention: Supporting young children with special needs and their families*. Baltimore, MD: Paul H. Brookes.

Meadan, H., & Daczewitz, M. E. (2015). Internet-based intervention training for parents of young children with disabilities: A promising service-delivery model. *Early child Development and Care, 185*, 155–169.

Meadan, H., Meyer, L. E., Snodgrass, M. R., & Halle, J. W. (2013). Coaching parents of young children with autism in rural areas using internet-based technologies: A pilot program. *Rural Special Education Quarterly, 32*, 3–10.

Poulou, M. S. (2015). Emotional and behavioural difficulties in preschool. *Journal of Child and Family Studies, 24*, 225–236.

Powell, D., & Dunlap, G. (2010). *Family-Focused Interventions for Promoting Social-Emotional Development in Infants and Toddlers with or at Risk for Disabilities*. Tampa, FL: Technical Assistance Center on Social Emotional Intervention for Young Children.

Powell, D., Fixsen, D., Dunlap, G., Smith, B., & Fox, L. (2007). A synthesis of knowledge relevant to pathways of service delivery for young children with or at risk of challenging behavior. *Journal of Early Intervention, 29*(2), 81–106.

Ruble, L. A., Dalrymple, N. J., & McGrew, J. H. (2010). The effects of consultation on individualized education program outcomes for young children with autism: The collaborative model for promoting competence and success. *Journal of early intervention, 32*(4), 286–301.

Rush, D. D., & Shelden, M. L. (2011). *The early childhood coaching handbook*. Baltimore, MD: Paul H. Brookes.

Salisbury, C., Woods, J., Snyder, P., Moddelmog, K., Mawdsley, H., Romano, M., & Windsor, K. (2017). Caregiver and provider experiences with coaching and embedded intervention. *Topics in Early Childhood Special Education*. Advanced online publication.

Smith, A. (2017). Record shares of Americans now have smartphones, have home broadband. *FactTank*. Washington, DC: Pew Research Center.

Effectiveness and Usability of a Self-Administered Parent Training Intervention for Building Social-Emotional Competence Among At-Risk Preschoolers

Rebecca N. Thomson and John S. Carlson

Abstract

Research Findings: Using a non-concurrent, multiple-baseline design ($N = 3$) and supplemental interviews, the purpose of the present study was to explore the effectiveness and usability of the Devereux Early Childhood Assessment, Second Edition (DECA-P2) family guide (Mackrain & Cairone, 2013), carried out in a self-administered format across 8 weeks within an at-risk preschool population (e.g., Head Start). While a replicated treatment effect across all three cases was not documented, two children experienced improvements in social behavior following parents' participation in the intervention. The DECA-P2 self-administered parent training intervention demonstrated a high level of usability, as parents implemented the program with high integrity (i.e., above 80%) and all reported moderate to high levels of acceptability. *Implications for Research & Practice:* Results suggest that the DECA-P2 self-administered parent training intervention may be effective for some families; however, other families may need adaptations or additional supports to see significant changes. The intervention's high level of usability among a sample of at-risk families suggests that it is a useful way to engage families in the treatment process. Potential adjustments (e.g., intervention length, added components) that might increase effectiveness for certain families warrant further study, and a tiered model of service delivery for the DECA-P2 family guide should be considered to address families' unique needs.

***Keywords*: self-administered, parent training, social-emotional competence, early childhood, preschool**

The first five years of life are a critical period for social and emotional development (Sheridan et al., 2014). When social-emotional challenges present in young children, early intervention is recommended to prevent the development of clinically significant behavior problems that may require more costly and intensive supports/services (e.g., special education; Jones, Greenberg, & Crowley, 2015; McCabe & Altamura, 2011). Since young children's development is heavily influenced by their interactions with parents in the home setting (Sheridan et al., 2014), parent training programs have been developed for building children's social-emotional competence, and several have been identified as evidence-based early interventions (EBIs; e.g., Incredible Years, Triple P; Armstrong, Ogg, Sundman-Wheat, & Walsh, 2014). While EBIs exist, research shows that these programs are less effective and/or underutilized among children and families from low-income backgrounds due to numerous practical barriers (e.g., lack of knowledge about the availability of EBIs, difficulties with transportation, unable to access service due to time or insufficient insurance). These barriers lead to low rates of service access (20%) and high rates of attrition (50%) for low-income children experiencing mental health concerns (Atkins et al., 2006).

Given the influence of poverty on children's developmental outcomes, there is a high level of need for mental health services within low-income communities. Children living in poverty are exposed to significant risk factors (e.g., single or variable parental status, lack of daily routines, exposure to violence; Sheridan et al., 2014) on a daily basis. Without strong social-emotional skills, which serve as protective factors (LeBuffe & Naglieri, 2012), exposure to these risk factors further increases the likelihood of negative developmental outcomes (Sheridan et al., 2014). Not surprisingly, social-emotional challenges are reported to be higher among preschoolers from low-income backgrounds (approximately 20% to 25%; Brown, Copeland, Sucharew, & Kahn, 2012; Weitzman, Edmonds, Davagnino, & Briggs-Gowan, 2013), as compared with the general preschool population (10%–15%; McCabe & Altamura, 2011). Despite the need within this population, most current EBIs are structured as face-to-face treatments (Rotheram-Borus, Swendeman, & Chorpita, 2012), which minimizes access to low-income families who may be unable to participate in face-to-face sessions due to scheduling conflicts, transportation issues, cost, and/or availability of qualified mental health professionals (Atkins et al., 2006).

Self-Administered Interventions

To ensure that EBIs reach a broader population of consumers (including hard-to-reach populations, such as children living in poverty), Rotheram-Borus and colleagues (2012) suggest the need for disruptive innovations, or adaptations that make an EBI more cost-effective, accessible, and scalable, such as self-administered interventions. Self-administered interventions, delivered via written materials and/or multimedia (e.g., video, audio), are readily available, inexpensive, and can be implemented at any time that is convenient for the client. Some self-administered interventions simply aim to offer support (i.e., self-help books), while others teach self-management skills through step-by-step programs (i.e., instructional manuals). Self-administered interventions may be disseminated and/or delivered by educators, psychologists, physicians, paraprofessionals, or other professionals. With such a level of flexibility, self-administered treatment approaches may expand the reach of current EBIs by moving service provision closer to children's natural environments (Elgar & McGrath, 2003).

Self-administered interventions have the potential to maintain the same level of effectiveness as current EBIs for building social-emotional competence in early childhood (Elgar & McGrath, 2003), while also being more likely to improve usability. For instance, many of the practical barriers that low-income families face (e.g., insufficient time, scheduling problems, cost, difficulties with transportation) negatively impact their ability to complete mental health interventions with integrity (Atkins et al., 2006). Self-administered interventions, however, may increase treatment integrity by allowing low-income families to complete program requirements at a time that is most convenient and to be able to readily access program materials at no (or minimal) cost. Furthermore, self-administered interventions may be an acceptable treatment delivery format for families, given the high rate of self-help book purchases across the United States relative to participation in therapy (Rotheram-Borus et al., 2012).

Previous studies have explored the use of self-administered interventions for various mental health concerns (e.g., attention deficit/hyperactivity disorder [ADHD], sleep problems, depression, disruptive behavior) with many demonstrating effectiveness in randomized controlled trials (Elgar & McGrath, 2003). While there is evidence to show that some self-administered parent training programs are effective in improving child behavior (e.g., Triple P, Incredible Years; Markie-Dadds & Sanders, 2006; Webster-Stratton, Kolpacoff, & Hollinsworth, 1988; Webster-Stratton, 1990), this body of research remains relatively small, and some practical barriers remain among the self-administered interventions investigated to date. For instance, both the Triple P program and the Incredible Years require time-intensive facilitator training, costly materials, and ten weeks or more of treatment (Armstrong et al., 2014). Given these limitations, it is necessary to empirically investigate other self-administered parent training interventions for enhancing children's social-emotional competence and reducing behavior concerns.

Devereux Early Childhood Assessment, Second Edition (DECA-P2) Family Guide

One promising self-administered option is a family guide included within the DECA-P2 program, a comprehensive, strengths-based prevention program for building social-emotional competence in preschool children (LeBuffe & Naglieri, 2012). The DECA-P2 family guide, entitled *Promoting Resilience For Now and Forever*, is a 40-page informational booklet that provides parents and families with an understanding of healthy social and emotional development while offering useful strategies to support the development of social and emotional skills in young children. The family guide focuses on three areas of social-emotional competence: 1) initiative (e.g., encouraging interests, involving children in daily tasks), 2) self-regulation (e.g., naming and discussing feelings, having simple rules and being consistent), and 3) attachment/relationships (e.g., creating special hello and goodbye routines, showing children how to make friends; Mackrain & Cairone, 2013). Strengths of the guide include: a) its link to evidence-based assessment measures and classroom resources (LeBuffe & Naglieri, 2012), b) its shorter length and considerably lower cost than the self-administered manuals for other parent training programs (e.g., Incredible Years, Triple P; Armstrong et al., 2014), and c) the ease of dissemination to parents without the need for extensive training or ongoing supervision (Mackrain & Cairone, 2013).

Thomson and Carlson (2016) documented promising exploratory findings in a within-group pilot study ($N = 12$) of the DECA-P2 family guide implemented in a self-administered format within a primarily Head Start population. Children demonstrated increases in social-emotional competence and reductions in behavior concerns following parents' participation in the DECA-P2 parent training intervention. Furthermore, parents completed the program with high levels of integrity, and rated the program as being highly acceptable for addressing their child's needs. Given the positive results, a more methodologically-rigorous investigation was recommended in a manner that would allow establishing a causal relationship between the intervention and outcomes (Sheridan, 2014). The purpose of the present study was to investigate the effectiveness and usability of the DECA-P2 self-administered parent training intervention using a non-concurrent, multiple-baseline across participants design with supplemental interviews. Specific research questions included:

1. Is the DECA-P2 self-administered parent training guide an effective intervention for building social-emotional competence and reducing behavior concerns in three Head Start preschoolers from low-income backgrounds?

2. How usable (i.e., acceptable, feasible) is the DECA-P2 self-administered parent training guide when implemented by three parents of Head Start preschoolers from low-income backgrounds?

Method
Participants

Participants included parents ($N = 3$) of 4- to 5-year-old children enrolled in Head Start programs. All children demonstrated at-risk social-emotional development, as indicated by scores at least one standard-deviation below the mean on the DECA-P2 Total Protective Factors (TPF) scale or one or more of the individual DECA-P2 TPF subscales (LeBuffe & Naglieri, 2012). Parent 1 was a 48-year-old biological father who identified as Latino/Hispanic. He was married, had obtained a high school diploma/GED, and was not working by choice (i.e., due to a disability). Child 1 was a 5-year-old male of mixed race/ethnicity. Parent 2 was a 25-year-old biological mother who identified as Black/African American. She was living with a significant other, had obtained a college degree, and was working full-time. Child 2 was a Black/African American 4-year-old female. Parent 3 was a 24-year-old biological mother who identified as White/Caucasian. She was living with a significant other, had obtained a high school diploma/GED, and was working part-time. Child 3 was a White/Caucasian 4-year-old male. All participating families were living in poverty, as indicated by annual household incomes below the federal poverty line.

Measures
Effectiveness

Direct Behavior Rating (DBR). DBRs (e.g., Riley-Tillman, Chafouleas, Sassu, Chanese, & Glazer, 2008) were used as the primary measure of child behavior (i.e., social-emotional competence, behavior concerns). Parents completed DBR ratings using an 11-point scale (ranging from 0 [*Never*] to 10 [*Always*]) for four behaviors: 1) "My child showed initiative today/this week" (e.g., tried new things, asked questions, stuck with a task even when it was hard to do), 2) "My child showed self-control today/this week" (e.g., calmed down when upset, listened to others, showed patience), 3) "My child interacted well with peers and adults today/this week" (e.g., showed affection for familiar adults, appeared happy when playing with others), and 4) "My child showed problem behaviors today/this week" (e.g., difficulty concentrating, hurt others with actions or words, temper tantrums). An average social-emotional competence score was determined by computing the mean of the first three items on the DBR form (i.e., items measuring initiative, self-regulation, and attachment/relationships). Higher scores for the average social-emotional competence DBR score indicate stronger social-emotional competence, and lower scores on the behavior concerns DBR item indicate fewer behavior concerns. DBRs have been found to significantly correlate with systematic direct observation (Riley-Tillman et al., 2008) and behavior rating scales (i.e., Social Skills Rating System; Chafouleas, Kilgus, & Hernandez, 2009), indicating strong convergent validity. Additionally, DBRs have demonstrated strong temporal reliability with only a small number of ratings (e.g., 2 to 10; Kilgus, Riley-Tillman, Stichter, Schoemann, & Bellesheim, 2016), as well as sensitivity to behavior change (Chafouleas, Sanetti, Kilgus, & Maggin, 2012).

Devereux Early Childhood Assessment – Second Edition (DECA-P2) rating scale (LeBuffe & Naglieri, 2012). The DECA-P2 rating scale, a 38-item strengths-based assessment for preschool children between the ages of 2 and 5, was used as a supplemental measure of child behavior. Social-emotional competencies are examined through the 27-item Total Protective Factors (TPF) scale, which is further divided into three subscales: Initiative, Self-Regulation, and Attachment/Relationships. On the TPF scale (and each of the subscales), T-scores of 60 or above represent a *Strength*, scores between 41 and 59 represent *Typical* functioning, and scores of 40 or below represent an *Area of Need*. Behavior concerns (BC) are assessed through an 11-item screener. On the BC scale, scores of 59 and below are considered *Typical* and scores of 60 or above are considered an *Area of Need*. The DECA-P2 demonstrates strong psychometric properties (e.g., internal consistency ≥ .80 for both scales, test-retest reliability ≥ .78 for both scales; LeBuffe & Naglieri, 2012).

Usability

Weekly integrity checklist. Parents completed a researcher-developed integrity checklist at the end of each intervention week by circling "Yes" or "No" to indicate whether they completed each of the intervention components. Treatment integrity was reflected by the percentage of intervention components parents reported completing out of the total number of intervention components.

Treatment Evaluation Questionnaire – Parent Form (TEQ-P; Kratochwill, Elliott, Loitz, Sladeczek, & Carlson, 2003), Acceptability Scale. Parents completed the acceptability scale of the TEQ-P (Kratochwill et al., 2003), which includes 11 items that are rated using a 6-point Likert-type scale ranging from 1 (*Strongly Disagree*) to 6 (*Strongly Agree*). Total scores on the TEQ-P acceptability scale range from 11 to 66, and scores of 55 and above are considered to reflect high acceptability (Kratochwill et al., 2003). The TEQ-P revealed strong internal consistency in the present study ($\alpha = .94$).

Open-ended interview. An open-ended interview at the final home visit was used to gather qualitative information about the acceptability of the intervention. Parents were asked three questions: 1) What were the best aspects of the program? 2) What aspects did you not like or not find helpful? and 3) How could the program have been improved to help you more?

Procedures

Recruitment. Participants were recruited from Head Start centers across five counties via phone blasts, parent newsletters, in-person presentations, and flyers. To qualify for participation in the study, children needed to be: 1) rated with T-scores between 28 and 40 on the DECA-P2 TPF scale or one or more of the TPF subscales (indicating that this was an *Area of Need*), 2) enrolled in a Head Start program, and 3) between 3 and 5 years of age at their last birthday. Parents needed to: 1) report an annual household income below the federal poverty line, and 2) speak English fluently.

Design. The present study followed a non-concurrent, multiple-baseline design across participants (with supplemental interviews).

Baseline (A). To promote internal validity, baseline phase lengths were determined a priori (between 5 to 9 days) and participants were randomly assigned to a baseline/treatment schedule upon enrolling in the study (Christ, 2007). During the baseline phase, parents completed the primary measure (i.e., DBR) daily and the supplemental measure (i.e., DECA-P2 rating scale) three times total. Parents received a monetary incentive of $25 at the end of the baseline phase.

Intervention (B). The intervention followed the chapters of the DECA-P2 family guide (Mackrain & Cairone, 2013) over an 8-week implementation period. Each week, an accompanying workbook instructed parents to: 1) read or review short sections from the family guide, 2) answer written questions to reflect on the content (e.g., "Describe a recent problem that you had a difficult time solving. What made the problem so tricky?"), 3) review three focus strategies, 4) brainstorm ideas for using the strategies in their daily life (e.g., "Which of your own feelings might you discuss with your child?"), and 5) use the three strategies as many times as possible. Parents could complete the readings, answer the written questions, and implement the strategies at their convenience during the week. At the end of each week, parents completed the primary measure (i.e., DBR) along with the Weekly Integrity Checklist. These data were submitted weekly to researchers via phone or e-mail. Home visits were conducted at the end of each of the three intervention modules (i.e., Initiative [Weeks 1–3], Self-Regulation [Weeks 4–6], Attachment/Relationships [Weeks 7–8]), during which parents completed the supplemental measure (i.e., DECA-P2 rating scale). Parents received a monetary incentive of $25 at each of the three home visits following each intervention module (for a total incentive of $100 across the baseline and intervention phases).

Post-test. Upon completion of the 8-week intervention, parents completed the TEQ-P acceptability scale and participated in an open-ended interview.

Follow-up. Four weeks after completing the 8-week intervention, parents were contacted via phone or e-mail and asked to complete the primary outcome measure (i.e., DBR).

Results

Effectiveness

A combination of visual and statistical analyses was used (Heyvaert & Onghena, 2014) to assess the effectiveness of the DECA-P2 self-administered parent training program. The first author and an undergraduate research assistant reviewed graphs of DBR scores using the visual analysis procedures outlined by Kratochwill and colleagues (2010; $\kappa = 1.00$). Statistical analysis included the Wampold and Worsham (1986) randomization test (calculated using the *ExPRT* [*Excel Package of Randomization Tests*] program; Levin, Evmenova, & Gafurov, 2014) and Tau-U effect size calculations (calculated using an online software program www.singlecaseresearch.org). Clinical significance was assessed using the RCI (Jacobson & Truax, 1991) for DECA-P2 rating scale scores.

Child social-emotional competence. Average social-emotional competence DBR scores (i.e., the primary measure) were graphed, and visual analysis did not find evidence of an intervention effect for any of the three participants (see Figure 1). Statistical analysis confirmed that there was not a significant change in social-emotional competence from baseline to intervention. The Wampold and Worsham (1986) randomization test was not significant ($p = .217$), suggesting that any changes in parent DBR ratings of social-emotional competence were not likely due to the intervention. Tau-U effect size calculations for average social-emotional competence DBR scores were non-significant for all three participants (see Table 1). Analysis of DECA-P2 TPF scores (i.e., the supplemental measure) did not suggest statistically significant changes in children's social-

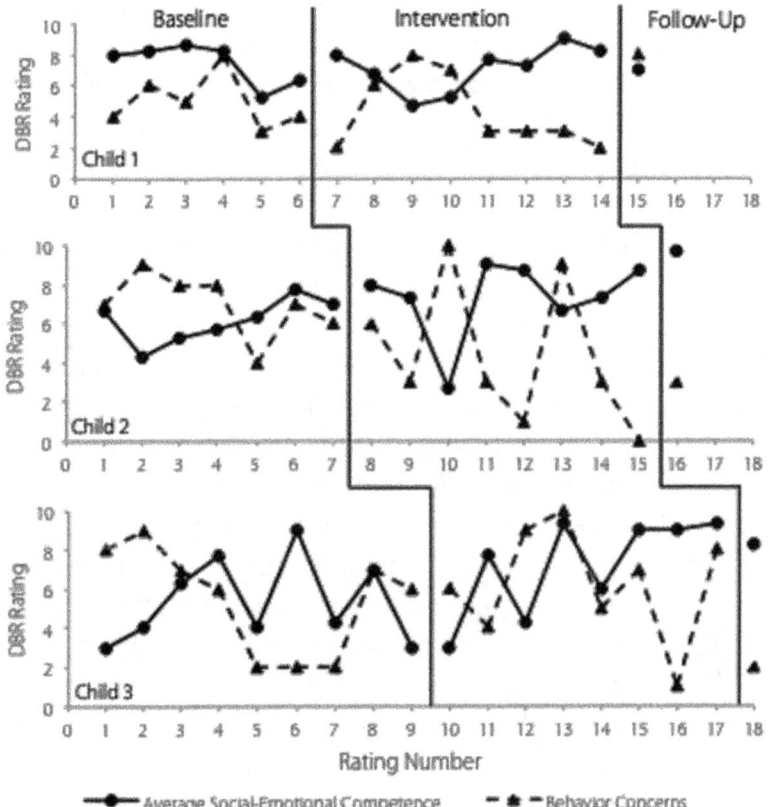

Figure 1 Parent DBR Ratings – Average Social-Emotional Competence and Behavior Concerns

Note. Average Social-Emotional Competence scores reflect the mean of the first three behaviors on the DBR form (i.e., Initiative, Self-Regulation, Attachment/Relationships). Behavior Concerns scores reflect the rating for the fourth behavior on the DBR form.

emotional competencies from baseline to intervention, though there was some evidence of clinically significant changes. Tau-U effect size calculations for DECA-P2 TPF scale scores were non-significant for all three participants (see Table 1). RCI calculation indicated a reliable increase (i.e., a larger change than what would be expected due to unreliability of a measure) in average DECA-P2 TPF scale scores for Child 2 (RCI = 4.25) and Child 3 (RCI = 3.00). Follow-up parent DBR ratings of social-emotional competence (4 weeks post-intervention) revealed an increase (i.e., improvement) from the intervention phase for Child 2 and Child 3, and a score decline for Child 1 (see Figure 1).

Child behavior concerns. Parent DBR ratings of behavior concerns (i.e., the primary measure) were graphed, and visual analysis did not find evidence of an intervention effect for any of the three participants (see Figure 2). Statistical analysis confirmed that there was not a significant change in behavior concerns from baseline to intervention. The Wampold and Worsham (1986) randomization test was not significant for average behavior concern scores ($p = .533$), indicating that the DECA-P2 self-administered parent training intervention did not have a significant influence on children's problem behaviors. Tau-U effect size calculations for behavior concern DBR scores were non-significant for all three participants (see Table 1). Analysis of DECA-P2 BC scale scores did not suggest any statistically significant changes in children's behavior concerns from baseline to intervention, though one child experienced a clinically significant decrease in behavior concerns. Tau-U effect size calculations for DECA-P2 BC scale scores were non-significant for all three participants (see Table 1). RCI calculation indicated a reliable decrease in average BC scale scores for Child 2 (RCI = 2.85). Follow-up parent DBR ratings of behavior concerns (4 weeks post-intervention) showed a decrease (i.e., improvement) from the level in the intervention phase for Child 2 and Child 3, and an increase in score for Child 1.

Table 1
Means and Effect Sizes for Measures of Child Social-Emotional Competence and Behavior Concerns

Measure/Child	Baseline M (SD; Range)	Intervention M (SD; Range)	M Change	Tau-U	p	RCI
Primary measure: DBR						
Average social-emotional competence						
Child 1	7.50 (1.35; 5.3-8.7)	7.13 (1.49; 4.7-9.0)	-.37	-.21	.519	–
Child 2	6.14 (1.12; 4.3-7.7)	7.29 (2.03; 2.7-9.0)	+1.15	.39+	.203	–
Child 3	5.37 (2.18; 3.0-9.0)	7.21 (2.48; 3.0-9.3)	+1.84	.47	.102	–
Average	**6.34 (1.08; 5.37-7.50)**	**7.21 (.08; 7.13-7.29)**	**+.87**	**.23**	**.193**	–
Behavior concerns						
Child 1	5.00 (1.79; 3-8)	4.25 (2.38; 2-8)	-.75	-.31	.333	–
Child 2	7.00 (1.63; 4-9)	4.38 (3.62; 0-10)	-2.62	-.46	.133	–
Child 3	5.44 (2.74; 2-9)	6.25 (2.92; 1-10)	+.81	.35+	.229	–
Average	**5.81 (1.05; 5.00-7.00)**	**4.96 (1.12; 4.25-6.25)**	**-.85**	**-.13**	**.465**	–
Supplemental measure: DECA-P2						
Total protective factors (TPF) T-score						
Child 1	44.33 (1.53; 43-46)	44.00 (6.08; 37-48)	-.33	.33	.513	.08
Child 2	37.00 (13.08; 28-52)	54.00 (19.16; 32-67)	+17.00	.78	.127	4.25*
Child 3	29.67 (1.53; 28-31)	41.67 (16.50; 28-60)	+12.00	.44	.383	3.00*
Average	**37.00 (7.33; 29.67-44.33)**	**46.56 (6.55; 44.00-54.00)**	**+9.56**	**.52**	**.078**	**2.39***
Behavior concerns (BC) T-score						
Child 1	61.00 (4.58; 56-65)	61.67 (3.21; 58-64)	+.67	.11	.827	.11
Child 2	71.33 (1.15; 70-72)	53.33 (17.24; 38-72)	-18.00	-.56	.275	2.85*
Child 3	72.00 (0; 72-72)	61.67 (12.34; 48-72)	-10.33	-.67	.190	1.63
Average	**68.11 (6.17; 61.00-72.00)**	**58.89 (4.81; 53.33-61.67)**	**-9.22**	**-.37**	**.208**	**1.46**

*p < .05. +Corrected for baseline trend

Usability

Integrity. Average integrity scores across the 8 weeks of the intervention were 80% or higher for all three participants (Parent 1: 86%; Parent 2: 80%; Parent 3: 93%), which reflects a high level of treatment integrity (Perepletchikova & Kazdin, 2005). Specifically, Parent 1 reported high integrity (i.e., above 80%) for 4 of the 8 weeks of the intervention, Parent 2 reported high integrity for 6 of the 8 weeks, and Parent 3 reported high integrity for 7 of the 8 weeks. Overall treatment integrity (across participants and weeks) averaged 86%.

Acceptability. Parents found the DECA-P2 self-administered parent training guide to be moderately-to-highly acceptable. A score of 55 or higher on the TEQ-P acceptability scale indicates an intervention is highly acceptable (Kratochwill et al., 2003), and Parent 1 and Parent 3's ratings exceeded this standard (Parent 1 Total Score: 58; Parent 3 Total Score: 65). Parent 2's rating was slightly below the standard for high acceptability (Total Score = 52). Open-ended interview responses provided additional information about the acceptability of the program (see Table 2 for specific responses). Parents primarily offered positive reflections about the program (e.g., "everything was helpful and enjoyable" [Parent 1], "helpful reminder of parenting strategies" [Parent 2], "made ideas about parenting more fresh in my mind" [Parent 3]). Aspects of the program that parents found to be challenging/unhelpful included the following: 1) scheduling time for reading (Parent 2), and 2) some repetitiveness in the workbook and questionnaires (Parent 2, Parent 3).

Discussion

The purpose of the present study was to examine the effectiveness and usability of a self-administered parent training intervention with the potential to improve family engagement in the development of social-emotional competence in early childhood. While there was not replicated evidence supporting the effectiveness of the DECA-P2 parent training intervention across all three participants, there were some individual clinically significant improvements documented for Child 2 (i.e., reliable increase in social-emotional competence; reliable decrease in behavior concerns) and Child 3 (i.e., reliable increase in social-emotional competence). Additionally, there were positive outcomes related to the usability of the intervention (i.e., integrity, acceptability).

Effectiveness

The response variation documented in the present study points to the need to consider individual characteristics and needs when exploring the usability and effectiveness of interventions in real-world settings. One potential reason that significant changes in child behavior were not documented consistently in the present study is that there was not much room for improvement in children's social-emotional competence. For instance, children's mean DBR ratings of social-emotional competence ranged from 5.37 to 7.50 (out of 10) during the baseline phase and two children's DECA-P2 TPF scale T-scores were in the *Typical* range at the initial rating. While all children met LeBuffe and Naglieri's (2012) criteria for at-risk social-emotional development, two of the three children (Child 1, Child 2) only demonstrated need in one area of social-emotional competence (i.e., self-regulation), rather than more global deficits in social-emotional functioning. In contrast, both the pilot study of the DECA-P2 self-administered parent training intervention (Thomson & Carlson, 2016) and previous studies of self-administered parent training programs (e.g., Incredible Years, Triple P) included children with greater overall levels of need (e.g., Markie-Dadds & Sanders, 2006; Webster-Stratton et al., 1988; Webster-Stratton, 1990), which allowed more room to see improvement.

Another potential reason that the DECA-P2 self-administered parent training intervention may not have been an effective program for all three families was that some may have required more intensive support. While the program instructs parents to practice the three focus strategies each week as "homework," parents do not have the opportunity to troubleshoot any challenges

Table 2
Parent Responses to Open-Ended Interview Questions

1. What were the best aspects of the program?	"The whole thing! Particularly liked the home visit aspect of the program" (Parent 1) "Helpful reminder of parenting strategies" (Parent 2) "The theory behind each strategy was interesting to read about and was helpful for conceptualization/brainstorming" (Parent 2) "Home visits were a source of excitement for the child" (Parent 2) "Doing the program made ideas about parenting more fresh in my mind, which led to better parenting practices" (Parent 3) "Allowed me to slow down and take time to do things with the kids" (Parent 3) "Questions were asked about the adult's life as well as the child's life" (Parent 3)
2. What aspects did you not like or not find helpful?	"No suggestions at the moment" (Parent 1) "An electronic format for the book would have been helpful" (Parent 2) "More clear exchange of contact information at the beginning would have been helpful" (Parent 3)
3. How could the program have been improved to help you more?	"Nothing! Everything was helpful and enjoyable to work on with the kids" (Parent 1) "It was sometimes difficult to find time to sit down and read" (Parent 2) "Questionnaires were organized in a confusing way or had repetitive questions" (Parent 2) "Sometimes repetitive, particularly in the workbook activities" (Parent 3)

or receive feedback from professionals about their performance, which may impact the accuracy and/or consistency of strategy implementation. Other studies of self-administered parent training programs have attempted to enhance the interventions by including scheduled phone consultation with a therapist (Markie-Dadds & Sanders, 2006) and the option to call the therapist anytime throughout the intervention period (Webster-Stratton, 1990). These enhancements were beneficial and could be a way to boost the effectiveness of the DECA-P2 self-administered parent training intervention. Additionally, the present intervention was several weeks shorter than other self-administered parent training interventions (e.g., Incredible Years, Triple P), which are typically between 10 and 12 weeks in length (Markie-Dadds & Sanders, 2006; Webster-Stratton et al., 1988; Webster-Stratton, 1990). Given that follow-up DBRs (i.e., 4 weeks post-intervention, which equates to the 12-week mark) showed continued improvement in child behavior for two of the three children in the present study (Child 2, Child 3), it may be that a few extra intervention weeks would allow time for changes to reach statistical significance.

Usability

Integrity. On average, parents who participated in the DECA-P2 self-administered parent training intervention reported 86% integrity to the intervention components, which is considered a high level of treatment integrity according to the standard suggested by Perepletchikova and Kazdin (2005; i.e., 80% or higher). This finding is similar to previous work, which has documented moderate (i.e., 71%) to high levels of treatment integrity with the use of the Incredible Years self-administered parent training program (Kratochwill et al., 2003; Ogg & Carlson, 2009) and high integrity (i.e., 95%) with the use of the DECA-P2 self-administered parent training intervention (Thomson & Carlson, 2016). The overall high level of parent-reported integrity in the present study suggests that the intervention components (e.g., reading, written questions, use of strategies) are feasible for families to implement within the context of the home setting, which is an essential prerequisite for disseminating EBIs in applied contexts.

Acceptability. All three parents rated the DECA-P2 self-administered parent training intervention as acceptable. Two parents (Parent 1, Parent 3) rated it as being highly acceptable, and one parent (Parent 2) rated it as being moderately acceptable, which mirrors the high acceptability found in the pilot study of the DECA-P2 self-administered parent training intervention (Thomson & Carlson, 2016) and in other studies of self-administered parent training interventions (e.g., Incredible Years; Kratochwill et al., 2003). Interview responses suggested that parents found the content and format of the intervention to be helpful. Parents generally reported that the DECA-P2 family guide was a fair, appropriate, and effective intervention to build their children's social-emotional competence, which is an important indicator of the transportability of the intervention into real-world contexts. Parent 2 and 3 appreciated the reminders of helpful parenting practices and how the guide required them to think more deeply about the parent strategies they were using. Suggestions for improvement included the use of an electronic format (i.e., web-based) and greater efficiency in content (i.e., less repetition).

Limitations

The present study is limited by: 1) issues with the reliability, validity, and sensitivity of the primary outcome measure, and 2) the use of parent-reported data to measure integrity. First, despite literature supporting the reliability and validity of DBRs (e.g., Chafouleas et al., 2009; Kilgus et al., 2016; Riley-Tillman et al., 2008), research has not been conducted on the psychometric properties of parent-rated DBRs. It is likely that teachers and other professionals have more prior experience with DBR-like tools (e.g., Daily Behavior Report Card) than parents, so it is unclear whether parent-rated DBRs are as reliable and valid as what is documented in the literature. Furthermore, ceiling effects (i.e., caused by relatively high scores at baseline) may have limited the sensitivity of the DBR measure. Finally, relying solely on a parent-reported measure to assess integrity is insufficient and may have led to biased or inaccurate reporting.

Implications for Research & Practice

Future research of the DECA-P2 self-administered parent training intervention should seek to: 1) explore the effectiveness and usability of the intervention with a slightly different target population (e.g., parents of young children with identified disabilities), and 2) test the potential benefit of some modifications/extensions to the intervention. First, inclusion criteria should be adjusted to include children with more problematic behavior and parents with more maladaptive parenting practices. While the DECA-P2 resources are intended for at-risk children and families (LeBuffe & Naglieri, 2012), it would be easier to establish a stable baseline pattern and/or show significant change if participants with more problematic behaviors were included (Boyle et al., 2010). Second, modifications/extensions may include increasing the intervention length (i.e., to 10 to 12 weeks) and/or phone/telehealth consultation with a therapist. All future research should aim to incorporate a primary outcome measure with greater reliability, validity, and sensitivity.

Practice

The present study informs practice by: 1) offering support for the usability (i.e., integrity, acceptability) of the DECA-P2 self-administered parent training intervention among hard-to-reach populations (i.e., families living in poverty), and 2) suggesting the potential need for a tiered model of service delivery, given the response variation among the participants. First, the usability of the intervention indicates that it can easily and efficiently be disseminated in real-world contexts in an effort to prevent the development of more significant problems and reduce the likelihood that children will need more intensive special education services. Second, the response variation (i.e., individual improvements only for Child 2 and Child 3) suggests that some families might benefit from a self-administered approach alone, while others may need additional supports (e.g., phone/telehealth consultation with a therapist, group discussion). Continued exploration of the DECA-P2 self-administered parent training intervention in applied settings will help to uncover whether any of these enhancements could be integrated into a tiered model of service delivery to address each family's unique level of need.

Funding statement: Funding for this research was provided by the Society for the Study of School Psychology (SSSP), the Michigan State University (MSU) Graduate School, and the MSU College of Education (Department of Counseling, Educational Psychology, and Special Education).

References

Armstrong, K. H., Ogg, J. A., Sundman-Wheat, A. N., & St. John Walsh, A. (2014). *Evidence-based interventions for children with challenging behavior.* New York: Springer.

Atkins, M. S., Frazier, S. L., Birman, D., Abdul Adil, J., Jackson, M., Graczyk, P. A., ... McKay, M. M. (2006). School-based mental health services for children living in high poverty urban communities. *Administration and Policy in Mental Health and Mental Health Services Research, 33,* 146–159. doi:10.1007/s10488-006-0031-9

Boyle, C. L., Sanders, M. R., Lutzker, J. R., Prinz, R. J., Shapiro, C., & Whitaker, D. J. (2010). An analysis of training, generalization, and maintenance effects of primary care Triple P for parents of preschool-aged children with disruptive behavior. *Child Psychiatry & Human Development, 41,* 114–131. doi:10.1007/s10578-009-0156-7

Brown, C. M., Copeland, K. A., Sucharew, H., & Kahn, R. S. (2012). Social-emotional problems in preschool-aged children: Opportunities for prevention and early intervention. *Archives of Pediatric & Adolescent Medicine, 166,* 926–932. doi:10.1001/archpediatrics.2012.793

Chafouleas, S. M., Kilgus, S. P., & Hernandez, P. (2009). Using direct behavior rating (DBR) to screen for school social risk: A preliminary comparison of methods in a kindergarten sample. *Assessment for Effective Intervention, 34,* 214–223. doi:10.1177/1534508409333547

Chafouleas, S. M., Sanetti, L. M., Kilgus, S. P., & Maggin, D. M. (2012). Evaluating sensitivity to behavioral change using direct behavior rating single-item scales. *Exceptional Children, 78,* 491–505. doi:10.1177/001440291207800406

Christ, T. J. (2007). Experimental control and threats to internal validity of concurrent and nonconcurrent multiple baseline designs. *Psychology in the Schools, 44,* 451–459. doi:10.1002/pits.20237

Elgar, F. J., & McGrath, P. J. (2003). Self-administered psychosocial treatments for children and families. *Journal of Clinical Psychology, 59,* 321–339. doi:10.1002/jclp.10132

Heyvaert, M., & Onghena, P. (2014). Randomization tests for single-case experiments: State of the art, state of the science, and state of the application. *Journal of Contextual Behavioral Science, 3,* 51–64. doi:10.1016/j.jcbs.2013.10.002

Jacobson, N. S., & Truax, P. (1991). Clinical significance: A statistical approach to defining meaningful change in psychotherapy research. *Journal of Consulting and Clinical Psychology, 59,* 12–19. doi:10.1037//0022-006X.59.1.12

Jones, D. E., Greenberg, M., & Crowley, M. (2015). Early social-emotional functioning and public health: The relationship between kindergarten social competence and future wellness. *American Jounral of Public Health, 105,* 2283–2290. doi:10.2105/AJPH.2015.302630

Kilgus, S. P., Riley-Tillman, T. C., Stichter, J. P., Schoemann, A. M., & Bellesheim, K. (2016). Reliability of direct behavior ratings – social competence (DBR-SC) data: How many ratings are necessary? *School Psychology Quarterly, 31,* 431–442. doi:10.1037/spq0000128

Kratochwill, T. R., Elliott, S. N., Loitz, P. A., Sladeczek, I., & Carlson, J. S. (2003). Conjoint consultation using self-administered manual and videotape parent-teacher training: Effects on children's behavioral difficulties. *School Psychology Quarterly, 18,* 269–302. doi:10.1521/scpq.18.3.269.22574

Kratochwill, T. R., Hitchcock, J., Horner, R. H., Levin, J. R., Odom, S. L., Rindskopf, D. M., & Shadish, W. R. (2010). *Single-case design technical documentation.* Retrieved from http://ies.ed.gov/ncee/wwc/pdf/wwc_scd.pdf

LeBuffe, P. A., & Naglieri, J. A. (2012). *Devereux early childhood assessment for preschoolers, second edition (DECA-P2): User's guide and technical manual.* Lewisville, NC: Kaplan Early Learning Company.

Levin, J. R., Evmenova, A. S., & Gafurov, B. S. (2014). The single-case data-analysis ExPRT (Excel package of randomization tests). In T. R. Kratochwill & J. R. Levin (Eds.), *Single-case intervention research: Methodological and statistical advances* (pp. 185–220). Washington, DC: American Psychological Association.

Mackrain, M., & Cairone, K. B. (2013). *Promoting resilience for now and forever: A family guide for supporting the social and emotional development of preschool children, second edition.* Lewisville, NC: Kaplan Early Learning Company. Markie-Dadds, C., & Sanders, M. R. (2006). A controlled evaluation of an enhanced self-directed behavioural family intervention for parents of children with conduct problems in rural and remote areas. *Behaviour Change, 23,* 55–72. doi:10.1375/bech.23.1.55

Markie-Dadds, C., & Sanders, M. R. (2006). Self-directed Triple P (Positive Parenting Program) for mothers with children at-risk of developing conduct problems. *Behavioural and Cognitive Psychotherapy, 34*(3), 259-275.

McCabe, P. C., & Altamura, M. (2011). Empirically valid strategies to improve social and emotional competence of preschool children. *Psychology in the Schools, 48,* 513–540. doi:10.1002/pits.20570

Ogg, J., & Carlson, J. S. (2009). The self-administered incredible years parent training program: Perceived effectiveness, acceptability, and integrity with children exhibiting symptoms of attention-deficit/hyperactivity disorder. *Journal of Evidence-Based Practices for Schools, 10,* 143–166.

Perepletchikova, F., & Kazdin, A. E. (2005). Treatment integrity and therapeutic change: Issues and research recommendations. *Clinical Psychology: Science and Practice, 12,* 365–383. doi:10.1093/clipsy.bpi045

Riley-Tillman, T. C., Chafouleas, S. M., Sassu, K. A., Chanese, J. A., & Glazer, A. D. (2008). Examining the agreement of direct behavior ratings and systematic direct observation data for on-task and disruptive behavior. *Journal of Positive Behavior Interventions, 10,* 136–143. doi:10.1177/1098300707312542

Rotheram-Borus, M. J., Swendeman, D., & Chorpita, B. F. (2012). Disruptive innovations for designing and diffusing evidence-based interventions. *American Psychologist, 67,* 463–476. doi:10.1037/a0028180

Sheridan, S. M. (2014). Single-case designs and large-N studies: The best of both worlds. In T. R. Kratochwill & J. R. Levin (Eds.), *Single-case intervention research: Methodological and statistical advances* (pp. 299–308). Washington, DC: American Psychological Association.

Sheridan, S. M., Knoche, L. L., Edwards, C. P., Kupzyk, K. A., Clarke, B. L., & Moorman Kim, E. (2014). Efficacy of the Getting Ready intervention and the role of parental depression. *Early Education and Development, 25,* 746–769. doi:10.1080/10409289.2014.862146

Thomson, R. N., & Carlson, J. S. (2016). A pilot study of a self-administered parent training intervention for building preschoolers' social-emotional competence. *Early Childhood Education Journal.* Advance online publication. doi:10.1007/s10643-016-0798-6

Wampold, B., & Worsham, N. (1986). Randomization tests for multiple-baseline designs. *Behavioral Assessment, 8,* 135–143.

Webster-Stratton, C. (1990). Enhancing the effectiveness of self-administered videotape parent training for families with conduct-problem children. *Journal of Abnormal Child Psychology, 18,* 479–492. doi:10.1007/BF00911103

Webster-Stratton, C., Kolpacoff, M., & Hollinsworth, T. (1988). Self-administered videotape therapy for families with conduct-problem children: Comparison with two cost-effective treatments and a control group. *Journal of Consulting and Clinical Psychology, 56,* 558–566. doi:10.1037/0022-006X.56.4.558

Weitzman, C., Edmonds, D., Davagnino, J., & Briggs-Gowan, M. J. (2013). Young child socioemotional/behavioral problems and cumulative psychosocial risk. *Infant Mental Health Journal, 35,* 1–9. doi:10.1002/imhj.21421

SPECIAL FOCUS II
Research in Community Childcare Programs

Introduction to the Special Focus: Research in Community Childcare Programs

Keri Giordano and Adrienne Garro

This special focus of Perspectives on Early Childhood Psychology and Education (PECPE) considers the unique needs of working in or collaborating with private, community childcare centers. Approximately 55–61% of children ages 3–5 attend formal early childhood programs (Child Trends Databank, 2014). Of these children, nearly 40% attend private childcare centers (Laughlin, 2013). The number of children under age 3 attending private centers is even higher as, with the exception of Early Head Start, publicly funded programs do not support children in this age group.

Despite the high number of children attending private childcare, it is much more common to find research focusing on state-funded early-learning programs or Head Start centers. This is concerning because the needs in private childcare centers are very different. Childcare staff tend to be undereducated, underpaid, and have a high rate of staff turnover. This, in combination with relatively low licensing standards, makes it a difficult setting when conducting and applying research.

This issue presents four research studies conducted in community childcare settings. Giordano, Martin, and Cornell examine an intervention that combines communities of practice with coaching to enhance the quality of child care center administrators. Lokteff and Austin use quality improvement rating scale data to describe factors that impact that quality of infant and toddler classrooms. Davis, Shivers, and Perry discuss the impact of early childhood mental health consultation on young boys of color. Finally, Garro, Pess, and Rittenhouse-Young present data from a research study focusing on childcare teachers' knowledge and perceptions of evidence-based practice and behavioral interventions.

While the focus of each study is distinct in terms of population examined and research questions addressed, together they begin to provide a foundation in understanding factors that affect quality of community-based early-learning programs. It is the hope of the guest editors that this special focus will both inform and inspire researchers to expand research, collaboration, and use of evidence-based practices in the private childcare community.

References

Child Trends Databank. (2014). *Early childhood program enrollment.* Retrieved from: https://www.childtrends.org/indicators/early-childhood-program-enrollment

Laghlin, L. (2013). Who's minding the kids? Child care arrangements: Spring 2011. *Current Population Reports, P70–135.* U.S. Washington DC: Census Bureau. Retrieved from: https://www.census.gov/prod/2013pubs/p70-135.pdf

Intentional Leadership: Utilizing Communities of Practice & Coaching Intervention to Support Professional Development of Early Childhood Program Administrators

Keri Giordano, Arlene Martin, and Kim M. Cornell

Abstract

The quality of an early learning program is ultimately linked to the quality of that program's leaders. Unfortunately, these leaders are often not prepared for their roles (Lieberman, 2017; McCormick Center, 2018). Communities of Practice (CoPs) and coaching interventions have received support as effective professional development methods for early childhood professionals (Biddle, 2012; Joyce & Showers, 2002; Kuh, 2012; Noble, 2008; Wenger & Wenger-Traynor, 2015). The current study examined the effects of a combined CoP and coaching intervention on a group of 20 administrators in early childhood settings. Participants took part in coursework needed to obtain an administrator credential. The group met weekly for 6-months and received support from the course instructor and a coach. Results suggest that the combined use of CoPs and coaching during academic instruction is an effective method of supporting early childhood administrators. Participants increased their readiness to change (as measured by the Stages of Change Scale), experienced enhanced program quality (as measured by the overall Program Administration Scale), and successfully obtained the administrator credential. Future work is needed to examine the long-term sustainability of changes made as a result of these supports.

Keywords: early childhood education, leadership, communities of practice, professional development, coaching

In the movement for quality early childhood programs, leadership development is slowly rising to the forefront of the agenda. On a national level, President Obama's 2014 Invest in Children early childhood funding initiatives first highlighted these issues. A major report from the Institute of Medicine (IOM) and the National Research Council (NRC), *Transforming the Workforce for Children Birth Through 8: A Unifying Foundation* (2015) describes the critical role that leadership plays in the elevation of the early childhood workforce. The quality of an early learning program is ultimately linked to the quality of that program's leaders. Unfortunately, these leaders are often undertrained and/or under-supported.

Lack of Preparation

Childcare administrators enter the role in a variety of ways. A recent study from the McCormick Center for Early Childhood Leadership indicated that 42% of center directors were previously teachers (2018). In this study, 24% of directors indicated that they became a director because others saw their potential and encouraged them to apply, while 15% said they were good teachers who were promoted to director positions. Other administrators are center owners or professionals with business or management training and no teaching experience. While each of these groups bring strong skill sets to the position, neither has been fully trained for the comprehensive role of program director, which requires business, management, and early education knowledge. The *Transforming the Workforce* report (IOM, 2015) lists competencies that leaders of early learning programs should have to be effective in their roles. These include skills related to child learning and assessment; ability to foster and guide the developing workforce; proficiency in assessing educators; ability to develop partnerships with staff, families, and other related professionals; and knowledge of fiscal and administrative management along with legal and regulatory requirements. Although there are approximately 3,000 early childhood undergraduate degree programs, only about 3% of those offer a concentration on leadership and management (Ferguson, 2017). New America's Early Learning and Elementary Education Policy Team conducted a scan of state requirements for early childhood administrators in the United States (Lieberman, 2017). Requirements for childcare-center directors were varied and standards typically fell short of expert recommendations. Two states and Washington DC require directors to have a minimum of a bachelor's degree, while seven do not require any formal education or training. Twenty-seven states do not require any prior work experience in childcare settings, if the director has obtained a certain level of formal education. While 30 states and Washington DC offer an administrator's credential for childcare center directors, only four require directors to obtain it. No states require formal performance evaluation of childcare-center directors. Given the lack of consistent education and training requirements, it is not surprising that 62% of directors indicated that they were not prepared when they first became an administrator (McCormick Center, 2018).

Communities of Practice (CoPs)

Communities of Practice (CoPs) are described as groups of professionals who meet on an ongoing basis with the goal of further developing their skills. Wenger and Wenger-Traynor (2015) discuss the three crucial characteristics of CoPs: domain, community, and practice. The group must share an area of interest (i.e., the domain) and, in pursuit of furthering one's knowledge about that interest, support each other and share content and resources (i.e., the community). The goal is for members to grow as individuals as a result of their participation. Through the relationships that professionals develop as part of a CoP, they are able to share knowledge, innovate practices, and solve problems. CoPs are becoming more recognized as a form of professional development in the field of early childhood (Kuh, 2012; Noble, 2008).

Realizing the need for professional development for early childhood leaders, a statewide early childhood professional development organization reviewed the literature and developed a series of leadership inquiry-based learning initiatives (Biddle, 2012; Perry, Henderson, & Meier, 2012; Rath & Conchie, 2008; Wenger & Wenger-Traynor, 2015). This series focused on enhancing leaders' strengths through the development of relationships, participation in reciprocal learning, and reflection on practice (Biddle, 2012). In these learning initiatives, CoPs were used to engage directors in leadership development through participation in interactive and hands-on learning experiences. Anecdotal stories from participants suggested this approach provided meaningful professional learning experiences and that participants felt they became stronger, more powerful agents of change as a result. The organization began referring to this process as *emergent professional learning,* unscripted dialogue that intrigues, provokes, disputes, or affirms the group's thinking. Learning within the context of relationships with others led to deeper thinking and evolving professional learning.

Coaching

In the same way an athletic coach works with players to help them develop their skills, educational coaches support teachers and other professionals in the implementation of evidence-based practices into their daily work. Coaching provides early childhood administrators with first-hand authentic and individualized support as they work towards professional change. Joyce and Showers (2002) found that when participants listen to a presentation or lecture, no content is consistently implemented in daily practice. This number increases to 5% when participants have the opportunity to practice and receive feedback on the new information. However, when coaching is used to support implementation, 95% of content translates into consistent use in daily practice. When coaching was incorporated into leadership-building initiatives in the state, participants felt they were better able to attain their goals.

The Current Project

Having recognized that CoPs and coaching can have positive impacts on early childhood leaders, the researchers decided that these two strategies would be combined with an existing leadership project, the New Jersey Administrator's Credential (NJAC), to examine the outcomes. The NJAC was developed in 2009 and designed with evidence-based and adult-learning practices in mind to provide administrators with essential knowledge in management and leadership while documenting competency (Professional Impact New Jersey, 2016). As participants began the journey of completing the NJAC, it became clear that a missing component of the process was a system of support (e.g., coaching, mentoring, technical assistance, peer-to-peer support, etc.) that candidates deemed necessary to move to completion. Through dialogue with candidates and other stakeholders, the current project emerged. Supported by grant funding, the project examined how leaders become agents of change for capacity and systems building as well as the influences that improve practices of program administrators.

The current project examined the process of change that occurred during a 24-week leadership and management course taken by early childhood center administrators. The aim of this course was to build capacity and systems in the workforce by enhancing the leadership and management skills of administrators in early childhood settings. A developing model was formed and the concept of a coaching intervention delivered through a CoP was incorporated as part of this model (Biddle, 2012; Wenger & Wenger-Traynor, 2015). The model created groups of early childhood administrators who met weekly to discuss structured topics over the course of 6 months, with the larger goal of obtaining their NJ Administrators' Credential.

Methods

Procedures

Candidates for this project were recruited from across the state. In order to participate in the project, participants needed to: 1) be an administrator of a licensed early childhood program for at least one year, 2) have a Bachelor of Arts or Bachelor of Science degree, 3) be an active member in the state's early childhood registry, 4) have a minimum of one year experience working with children, and 5) not be participating in the state's quality rating program. Participants were provided with a full scholarship for the program, including the coursework, materials, and the coaching, and each received $500 upon being awarded the NJAC. Although approximately 50 candidates initially signed up for the group, state systems prevented administrators from dual participation in ongoing initiatives, leaving only 23 qualifying participants.

Coaches and instructors for the project were recruited from a known community. Three professionals chose to serve in the dual role of coach and instructor, one professional chose to serve in the instructor role only, and one professional chose to serve in the coach role only. These five professionals were assigned to four regional cohorts; three cohorts with the dual coach/instructor role and one cohort with the separate instructor and coach roles. Coaches and instructors were provided with intensive training, which included the credentialing process, a facilitation training for using a CoP, and assessment measures training.

Finally, coaches and instructors participated in four ongoing leadership CoP sessions during the project with the grant team. These leadership CoPs were meant to strengthen the connection among the team. Participation by the instructors and coaches also kept them in a parallel process to experience first-hand the process they were facilitating with their participants in the course. The leadership CoPs provided an opportunity to engage in reciprocal learning, strategize ways to address concerns with instruction or coaching, celebrate the successes along the way, share anecdotal stories, and adjust practices within the grant project.

All participant candidates received an on-site pre-assessment within the first 7 weeks of coursework. Course sessions were 6 hours each, held once per week for 20 weeks, totaling 120 hours of coursework. Coursework focused on the NJAC framework, which includes 21 topics related to the administration of early learning programs. During this time, coaches also provided 24 hours of one-on-one and group intervention support to candidates in the development of their program improvement plans and the creation of portfolios, which needed to be submitted in order to obtain the NJAC. Overall, candidate participants were involved in a total of 144 hours of professional learning. Prior to the end of the course (weeks 21–24), participants received an onsite post-assessment.

Sample

Candidates. Four CoP cohorts were established across four regions. A total of 23 candidate participants enrolled in the program and 20 completed the course. The majority (85%) of candidate participants were employed in the role of center director, while the remainder (15%) were employed as assistant directors. Two pairs (four candidates in total) were employed at the same site. Half (50%) worked in the field less than 3 years, while 25% worked in the field between 11 and 20 years. One candidate worked in the field for over 20 years. Most of the candidates reported having a bachelor's degree (70%), while 30% reported having a master's degree.

Membership in each cohort ranged from four to eight people. No participant candidate attended all sessions. Absences of those who completed the course ranged from one to four missed classes, with an average of 2.65 missed classes and a median of three classes. The mode was four missed classes (30% of all classes).

Instructors and coaches. Demographic data were collected on the five coaches and instructors involved in this project. The majority (four) had over 11 years of experience in administration of early learning programs; one had 6 years of experience. Two people worked in the field of early childhood for at least 17 years, while three worked in the field over 25 years. Two facilitated professional development for at least 17 years and three coach/instructors worked as coaches/instructors for over 30 years. In terms of education, three coach/instructors had master's degrees, one had a doctorate, and one had a bachelor's degree.

Measures

Stage of Change Scale (SOCS). The SOCS is a tool designed to measure one's readiness to change. Seven items are ranked on a 5-point scale, which examined an individual's behavior and attitude towards change. Results are calculated and the final score classified readiness to change on one of five levels: pre-contemplation, contemplation, preparation, action, and maintenance. The SOCS was used with 20 candidates. The SOCS was used by the session instructor during the 7th week of class and the 24th week of class to examine readiness to change.

Program Administration Scale (PAS). The Program Administration Scale (PAS) is a tool designed to assess leadership and management practices of early childhood programs. Twenty-five items are ranked on a 7-point scale. Results provide an overall PAS score, an average PAS-item score, and 10 subscale scores. Pre-PAS assessments were conducted within the first 7 weeks of classes and post PAS assessments were carried out between weeks 21 and 24 by nine individuals reliable as PAS assessors.

Reflective journaling. Each week, participant candidates, coaches, and instructors engaged in a guided reflective journaling experience. During class, candidates were provided with a form to guide their reflections for the week. The form consisted of three Likert-scale questions, one question where multiple answers could be selected, and three open-ended questions. The first three questions targeted candidates' thoughts and feelings towards their learning process each week. Candidates were asked to respond to each question on a 5-point scale, where 1 indicated "not at all" and 5 indicated "absolutely, very much." Candidates were next asked to select the greatest barriers to their growth as early childhood administrators. Finally, candidates were asked three open-ended questions reflecting on their weekly experiences. Depending on the instructor, candidates either completed this form at the end of the session or throughout the session. The same form was completed after each of the 24 sessions by all candidates.

Instructors/coaches also completed a weekly journal reflecting on each session. The instructor/coach journal form consisted of seven open-ended questions. This form mirrored the candidate form and expanded upon it to allow instructors and coaches to examine their own influences in the CoP process.

Final evaluations. During the final session, candidates were asked to complete a written evaluation of their credentialing experience. The form consisted of a combination of Likert scale questions and open-ended questions. Questions examined the influences of the instructor, coach, and members of the CoP cohort on commitment to the project. They also looked at ways in which candidates planned on utilizing content from this program as leaders in their own programs and the sustainability of practices learned after the program's end. Finally, some questions examined the quality of relationships developed as part of the program and the impact that those relationships had on success in the program and growth as a leader.

Results

Stage of Change Scale (SOCS)

Initial scores on the SOCS ranged from 3: Preparation Stage (85%) to 4: Action (15%). Most candidates (85%) were at Stage 3. All candidates started the program with an initial score of 3 or higher, which makes sense in that the actions of locating, registering for, and attending the program show that the participants have some readiness for change. Final SOCS scores varied from 3: Preparation Stage (15%), 4: Action (35%), and 5: Maintenance (50%). The results showed that 15 candidates (75%) moved up at least one level from where they started, and 9 candidates (45%) moved up two levels. Half of the candidates (50%) reached Stage 5 at the end of the coursework.

Program Administration Scale (PAS)

A total of 20 candidates participated in both pre- and post-PAS assessments. Nineteen candidates (95%) showed an increase in the overall PAS sum of items score and one candidate showed a slight decrease. Nineteen candidates (95%) also demonstrated an increase in the average PAS item score and one candidate showed no change.

Paired sample t-tests were conducted to examine the significance of this difference. Cohen's d was used to calculate effect size. When examining the total PAS score, a significant difference was found between pre- and post-assessments ($t = -6.601, p < .001$) and a large effect size was calculated (Cohen's $d = 1.588$). Similar results were found when comparing pre- and post-average item scores ($t = -6.575, p < .001$, Cohen's $d = 1.568$). See Table 1 for a review of the results. These results indicate that participation in CoP revolving around early childhood administrator credentialing supported by coaching increased aspects of the overall quality of early learning programs as measured by the PAS.

Paired sample t-tests were also used to examine the significance of change on individual items. Cohen's d was again used to calculate effect size. Twenty-one individual items were examined; items related to staff qualifications were not individually examined, as these qualifications were not directly addressed by this intervention.

Table 1
Pre- and Post-PAS Differences

	t-score	d	Pre-course PAS		Post-course PAS	
			M	SD	M	SD
Total Score	-6.601 *	1.588	59.68	21.45	84.62	27.71
Average Item Score	-6.575 *	1.568	2.57	0.88	3.50	1.11

* $p < .001$

Table 2
Pre- and Post- PAS Individual Items Differences

	t-score	d	Pre-course PAS M	Pre-course PAS SD	Post-course PAS M	Post-course PAS SD
Staff Orientation	5.23 ***	1.25	2.45	1.46	4.65	2.20
Supervision & Performance Appraisal	6.84 ***	1.64	2.05	1.40	4.15	1.90
Compensation	2.64 *	0.59	2.35	2.10	3.45	2.06
Risk Management	5.48 ***	1.41	1.85	1.15	3.95	2.09
Internal Communications	2.32 *	0.57	1.25	0.77	2.00	1.48
Assessment in Support of Learnng	3.39 **	0.76	2.85	2.17	3.65	2.15
Budget Planning	3.61 **	0.91	1.75	1.18	3.35	2.20
Accounting Practices	2.57 *	0.58	2.00	1.82	3.40	2.27
Program Evaluation	3.76 **	0.91	1.40	0.92	2.80	1.66
Family Communications	3.29 **	0.75	2.20	1.96	3.60	2.42
Family Support & Involvement	3.01 **	0.69	3.30	1.62	4.65	1.06
External Communications	3.07 **	0.69	3.10	1.67	4.60	1.74
Community Outreach	4.24 ***	0.94	3.20	1.78	4.55	1.40

* p < .05   ** p < .01   *** p < .01

Significant differences were found on 13 individual items (see Table 2). As part of the course, candidates each selected one area to focus on for their program improvement plans. Interestingly, of the 13 items that showed significant change only five were selected areas of focus by participants in their improvement plans. This indicates that, although candidates were intentionally focused on the process of improvement in one specific area, they demonstrated growth in several areas.

Reflective Journaling: Candidates

A total of 348 candidate journaling forms were reviewed. The forms span the 24-week course. The missing forms were due to student absences and students being unable to complete the reflection for a variety of reasons. Candidates were asked to respond to each question on a 5-point scale, where 1 indicates "not at all" and 5 indicates "absolutely, very much." The first question asked, "Has this week's session increased your learning?" Overall, the majority of candidates (74%) responded with 5 (absolutely, a lot), followed by 4 (yes, a lot) (15%). In all of the submitted journals, no candidate endorsed 1 (no, not at all) for any of the sessions, and only 6 candidates (2%) endorsed sessions as rating a 2 (yes, a little bit).

The second question asked if interactions with others enhanced learning. Again, the majority of respondents (79%) endorsed 5 (absolutely, a lot), followed by 4 (yes, a lot) (14%). A total of 6 people (6%) indicated that their learning was not enhanced by others or only enhanced a little bit. The third question asked if learning was hindered by others in the group. The majority (92%) indicated that their learning was not hindered by the group. While 5% indicated that their learning was absolutely hindered by the group, it is possible that some of these cases were from misreading the scale. For the first two questions, a rating of 5 indicates high satisfaction, while on the third question, a 1 indicates a high level of satisfaction. Based on other responses on the reflection sheet, it seems as if some candidates were endorsing a high level of satisfaction from learning within the group, despite indicating that others have absolutely hindered their learning.

Candidates were next asked to select the greatest barriers to their growth as early childhood administrators; more than one option could be selected. The two greatest endorsed barriers were time and money, with a lack of formal education in early childhood and federal, state, and local regulations receiving the least number of endorsements.

For the final portion of the journal, candidates were asked three opened-ended questions. Responses to these questions were reviewed and coded. The first question asked candidates to describe their biggest "a-ha" (eye opening) moment from the session. There was great variability in responses to this question, but some clear themes were found. The most common response to this question involved course content and/or candidate's professional portfolios. Responses directly related to the topic of the session (e.g., "I need a vision and mission") and/or specific to the content required for the portfolios (e.g., "I was able to complete three more assignments") were put into this category. Responses related to broader thoughts on the group and/or the process, or to prior courses were separately coded. Another strong theme that arose revolved around the idea of learning that is rooted in relationships and the ability to share ideas and experiences with others and to learn from others. One candidate reflected, "I love sharing and getting the wisdom from classmates." Although not as strong, four additional themes were expressed consistently by candidate participants over the course of the program. One theme focused on beginning to view themselves as agents of change. An additional theme revolved around feeling re-energized about their work after participating in this program. Finally, a theme of "I am not alone" was found in the responses.

The second open-ended question asked candidates to describe how their work as early childhood administrators changed as a result of participating in the sessions. Again, anything specifically related to the topic of the day's course and/or the portfolio was coded together, and the majority of responses revolved around this theme. Similarly, a focus on learning within the context of others and from the professional dialogue that occurred was found. Candidates consistently returned to this theme throughout the sessions, reflecting, "I have developed an informed peer support system to rely upon after this course is over. Their experiences and expertise have enhanced my work significantly."

Candidates also expressed an increasing sense of confidence and empowerment as a result of their participation in the sessions. One example read, "It continues to be a confidence builder for me. I am consistently observing and assessing my program and my abilities as a leader." Candidates discussed their increased organization and focus (e.g., "It has made me more organized—I have been able to accomplish more than I thought") as well as an enhanced sense of self-awareness and use of reflective practices (e.g., "It has enlightened me and forced me to open up and reflect on myself and my vision"). Finally, candidates discussed steps that they took to use what they learned to support staff. Responses that referred to intention to use content were coded differently than responses indicating actual use; the strong theme of specific action that has been taken was prevalent.

The final open-ended question asked candidates to discuss how they intended to apply content from the session in their future work. For this question, more so than the two prior questions, candidates strongly focused on strategies from the specific session and/or their portfolio. Two additional themes were prevalent in candidate's responses. The first revolved around inspiring or empowering others; this typically involved a focus on their staff. A related, but distinct theme of implementing communities of practice at participants' own sites was also found.

Reflective Journaling: Instructors and Coaches

Instructors/coaches also completed a weekly journal reflecting on each session. The instructor/coach journal consisted of seven open-ended questions. The first question asked instructors/coaches to share evidence of shifts in candidates' thinking. The most common response to this question was a focus on content from the session topic (e.g., "Today's discussion on learning environments invoked a variety of philosophies"). Two other themes involved a sense of reignited passion/renewed energy and description of more self-awareness. One reflection describes, "Candidates are beginning to think deeply about their program operations .... The more (they) find out (they) could do things differently with more success, the more inspired (they are) to go at it each day, with new energy."

When asked to reflect on how interactions among candidates enhanced learning, the most frequent responses involved the ongoing development of relationships, with comments reflecting on increased bonding, vulnerability, openness, and trust among group members. Other themes revolved around active participation by all members and the sharing of ideas, stories, and resources. Instructors and coaches were also asked to reflect on how candidates' learning was hindered by others. By far, the most frequent response was that learning was not at all hindered by others in the group. When asked to discuss the biggest barriers to the instruction/coaching, the majority of responses indicated that there were no barriers. When instructors/coaches did discuss barriers, they primarily involved candidate absences and lack of time (in the individual sessions and in the overall program). Similar to candidates, instructors/coaches were asked to describe their biggest "a-ha" (eye opening) moment from the session. The majority of these responses related to content from the specific session. Instructors/coaches also talked about seeing the effects of their instruction in candidates' work and about the genuine enjoyment of the session by candidates and instructors/

coaches. One coach/instructor wrote, "The biggest 'a-ha' moment from today was to see how motivated each of the participants is to share their [work]. The pride that they currently have in their work is exciting to see!"

Also in line with the candidates' reflections, instructors/coaches were asked to describe how their work as an instructor/coach changed as a result of the session and how they intend to apply something from the session in their practices. When examining the change in work, instructors/coaches talked about their own continued professional growth; specifically, they discussed the idea that coaching others increased their own professional skills. One coach/instructor reflected, "My knowledge and understanding continues to increase each week as I prepare for course discussions and conversations. I feel empowered and helpful." There were also themes of applying the content from the session to themselves as professionals and of the parallel process of the course content; instructors/coaches talked about using the topic from the day's session in their work with the candidates.

Final Evaluations

During the final session, candidates were asked to complete a written evaluation of their credentialing experience. The form consisted of a combination of Likert-scale questions and open-ended questions. A total of 20 candidates completed this evaluation. The first set of questions asked candidates to reflect on the impact of others on their experience. When asked about instructor impact, 95% of candidates indicated that the instructor had either a strong positive or a positive impact on their commitment to the credentialing process. The results were more varied when reflecting on the impact of the coach, with 75% indicating that the coach had a strong positive or positive impact, 15% that she had a neutral or no impact, and 10% responding that the coach had a negative impact. It is notable that the scores were more consistent within cohorts, which may indicate that some styles of coaching were a better match for this project and/or the candidates in the group. All candidates indicated that colleagues had either a strong positive or positive impact in their weekly commitment to the process. In this section, candidates were also presented with an open-ended question asking them to provide additional thoughts about the impact of others on their process. Candidates (45%) talked about how their relationships with others enhanced their experiences. One candidate said, "Our relationships enriched the experience tremendously. We visited each other's sites, collaborated on work issues, and encouraged each other."

The next section asked candidates to think about maintaining contact with others once the credentialing process has ended. More than half (65%) of respondents indicated that they were highly likely to maintain contact with their instructor, while a third (30%) said that they were either very likely or somewhat likely to do so. When thinking about contact with the coach, almost half (45%) indicated that they were highly likely to maintain contact, while the remainder said they were very likely (20%), not likely (20%) or unsure (15%). All candidates responded that they were highly likely or very likely to maintain contact with their colleagues. Most candidates (95%) also said that they were either highly likely or very likely to continue to schedule time to meet with their colleagues. Candidates indicated an intention to utilize the CoP approach model within their own programs with 90% responding that they were either highly likely or very likely to do so.

Collaborative practices and supports provided throughout the program were examined. All candidates responded that they collaborated with colleagues during the weekly sessions. They focused on the sharing of documentation, resources, and experiences from their own centers (e.g., "always shared resources; stories were very helpful; I made friends"). In addition, all candidates described collaborating with colleagues outside of weekly sessions though meetings, visiting each other's programs, texts, emails, and/or phone calls. Most candidates (70%) sought out individual contact with the instructor during class, and those that did typically did each week (40%).

The last set of structured questions asked about the sustainability of practices learned in the credentialing process. In response to these questions, candidates talked about a desire to continue work on overall center quality and PAS criteria. Candidates also talked about a desire to continue their own development and growth as a leader. Continuing to support and encourage the development of staff and a sense of self-confidence were also themes that were reported. One reflection reads, "I have grown as a professional in ways I didn't think possible. I will continue to make changes as a result of this program."

Course Completion & Credentials Awarded

All 20 candidates completed the coursework and submitted portfolios; 18 were awarded the administrator's credential. Of the two that were not awarded the credential, one candidate's Bachelor of Arts could not be validated (a requirement to receive the credential) and the other candidate did not re-submit components of the portfolio that required some rewriting and editing. It is important to note that this submission rate is higher than what has been found when the course was conducted without the CoP and coaching support. In this project, 100% of candidates submitted portfolios, while in previous cohorts, 20% typically submit. In addition to higher submission rates, the overall quality of portfolios was enhanced. In this project, 20% of submitted portfolios required re-writing and editing. In prior cohorts, this rate typically falls closer to 50%.

Discussion

This goal of this project was to examine how leaders become agents of change for capacity and systems building and to consider factors that improve practices of program administrators through a leadership program incorporating coursework, coaching, and CoPs. Overall, the results suggest that this combination of components increases the leadership abilities of professionals and their knowledge of quality practices. Participants in this group showed significant increases on PAS scores as well as increases in their readiness to change as measured by the SOCS. Eighteen candidates were awarded the NJAC indicating they have developed "leadership and management skills required of administrators to lead their early learning programs in assessing and building the level of quality, as well as advocate for quality care for all children and families" (Professional Impact New Jersey, 2016). When reflecting on their experiences in the process, candidates repeatedly discussed the positive influence relationships (both peer and coach/instructor) had on the process. Through these reflections, candidates demonstrated growth in both PAS practices and in themselves as leaders.

Future research in this area should focus on a larger sample and examine the long-term sustainability of change. Individual components (e.g., coaching, CoPs, financial incentives) should be examined to help determine the impact each has on the change process. Finally, further work must be done to determine if candidates who have engaged in this process can serve as role models to other early childhood administrators.

Implications

Ongoing, continuous professional preparation and development must include supports for early childhood administrators to become agents of change. The ability of the early childhood administrator to impart leadership, support, encouragement, and direction for the career development of their staff is also necessary. When leaders are engaged in CoPs that embrace strengths-based qualities, they are able to elevate their own professional goals. For example, one participant is now in a leadership position as a Board Member of an early childhood professional organization while two participants are offering child development associate coursework in-house to their staff members.

This project revealed that the PAS assessment tool can be used for strategic planning and continuous quality improvement by early childhood administrators. Through the course, they learned how to develop a program improvement plan (PIP) for one area of their PAS data. Through written reflections and telephone interviews, candidates indicated they will continue to make program and practice improvements by creating PIPs for low scoring areas of their PAS. Data also revealed that the impact of participating in a CoP for professional learning inspires early childhood administrators to use this approach with their staff to create authentic staff development.

In looking at ways to best inform the professional development of early childhood administrators within community childcare centers, this project identified CoPs grounded in principles of fostering relationship-based and reflective practices combined with coaching to be effective methods. If improved outcomes for children and higher quality childcare programs are desired, early childhood administrators need to improve their own self-awareness, reflective actions, and leadership skills. The project demonstrated that through inquiry, reflection, and social learning, community childcare administrators were able to become more competent leaders and to enhance the overall quality of their programs.

Limitations

There were several limitations which may have impacted the results of this project. First, due to participation restrictions, the cohort sizes were relatively small; a larger sample is needed in order to fully examine the effects of this method. Participants were also provided with financial incentive for completing the program; since this has not been done in the past, it may be that the incentive, rather than the interventions, enhanced portfolio completion. Some groups were led by one person serving as both the coach and instructor while others had separate people in these roles. Further examination is needed to determine if this influences the results. Since several supports were provided (i.e., financial incentives, coursework, coaching, and CoPs), it is difficult to determine which of these (or a combination of all or some) made the most impact. Also, although there is strong evidence of short-term change, this evaluation did not provide for examination of long-term change as a result of participation.

Authors' Note: This work was supported by The Nicholson Foundation.

References

Biddle, J. K. (2012). *The three Rs of leadership: Building effective early childhood programs through relationships, reciprocal learning, and reflection*. Ypsilanti, MI: HighScope Press.

Ferguson, D. (2017). Leadership development for center-based child care and early education program directors: Research-to-policy resources. *Child Care & Early Education Research Connections*. Retrieved from https://www.researchconnections.org/childcare/resources/34693/pdf

Institute of Medicine & National Research Council of the National Academies. (2015). *Transforming the workforce for children birth through eight: A unifying foundation*. Washington, DC: The National Academies Press.

Joyce, B. R., & Showers, B. (2002). *Student achievement through staff development* (3rd ed.). Alexandria, VA: Association for Supervision & Curriculum Development.

Kuh, L. (2012). Promoting communities of practice and parallel process in early childhood settings. *Journal of Early Childhood Teacher Education, 33*(1), 19–37.

Lieberman, A. (2017). A tale of two pre-k leaders: How state policies for center directors and principals leading pre-k programs differ and why they shouldn't. Washington, DC: New America. Retrieved from http://na-production.s3.amazonaws.com/documents/Tale-Two-PreK-Leaders.pdf

McCormick Center for Early Childhood Leadership. (2018). Director's professional development needs differ by developmental stage. *Research, Whole Leadership*. Retrieved from https://mccormickcenter.nl.edu/library directors-professional-development-needs-differ-by-developmental-stage/

Noble, K. (2008). Communities of practice: Innovation in early childhood education and care teacher and practitioner preparation. *International Journal of Learning, 14*(9), 133–138.

Perry, G., Henderson, B., & Meier, D. R. (Eds.). (2012). *Our inquiry, our practice: Undertaking, supporting, and learning from early childhood teacher research(ers)*. Washington, DC: NAEYC.

Professional Impact New Jersey. (2016). *NJ Administrators' credential: Guide for administrators and facilitators*. Union, NJ: PINJ.

Rath, T., & Conchie, B. (2008). *Strengths based leadership: Great leaders, teams, and why people follow.* New York, NY: Gallup Press.

Wenger, E., & Wenger-Traynor, B. (2015). *Introduction to communities of practice: A brief overview of the concept and its uses.* Retrieved from http://wenger-trayner.com/introduction-to-communities-of-practice/

Factors Associated with Global Quality Change in Infant and Toddler Child Care Programs

Maegan Lokteff and Ann Berghout Austin

Abstract

High quality infant and toddler child care has repeatedly been linked to better outcomes for children. However, in the United States, infant and toddler child care has also been plagued by poor quality especially in community-based or private centers. In an effort to increase the quality of care for infants and toddlers, federal funding from the Child Care Development Fund has been invested in quality improvement projects serving community and private programs. Framed in an ecological model that views quality as the product and interaction of process, structural, and caregiver characteristics, this study addressed the impact of these variables on quality change. The sample was comprised of 86 classrooms nested within 48 centers that participated in a state-wide quality improvement project. Data included *Infant and Toddler Environmental Rating Scale-Revised* (ITERS-R) scores, wages, turnover, geographic location, and parent fees collected between 2003 and 2010 as part of the *Quality Improvement Project*. A mixed model analysis was used to examine if quality changed over time and the factors associated with higher or lower quality classrooms. Results indicate that classroom *ITERS-R* scores did increase over time. Two factors appeared significant for contributing to higher or lower scores, specialized IT training and turnover. This paper discusses implications of these two factors as it relates to improving quality in community-based programs.

***Keywords*: infant/toddler child care, child care quality, turnover, professional development**

Introduction

Child Care Aware of America estimates that nearly 11 million children under the age of 5 are in some type of child care. Despite a growing number of public preschool programs that subsidize access for families with 3- and 4-year-olds, infants, and toddlers are still primarily cared for in diverse arrangements that include friend, family, and neighbor care as well as private or community-based centers. Since the groundbreaking 1995 report, *Cost, Quality, and Child Outcomes in Child Care Centers* (Helburn), which made clear that the quality of experiences for young children in community based centers was often mediocre and especially poor for infants and toddlers, funding from the federal Child Care and Development Block Grants has been set aside for states to address and improve quality in community-based programs. However, little is known about the impact this funding has had on actually improving global quality for children under the age of 3 or what factors may best explain why some programs are able to achieve quality improvement while others do not. Using a mixed model, this study provides a unique look at how center-based infant and toddler child care programs experienced quality change while participating in one western state's quality improvement project and the factors associated with change. This paper provides evidence of the importance of center and community characteristics that affect the quality of care infants and toddlers receive and a programs ability to improve that quality.

Literature Review

Quality in Infant and Toddler Childcare

Despite research indicating positive developmental outcomes for children receiving high-quality care and increasing numbers of young children in out-of-home care, infant and toddler programs are often plagued with poor structural and process quality and have the least prepared and lowest compensated workforce (Burchinal, Roberts, Nabors, & Bryant, 1996; Dennehy & Marshall, 2005; Gerber,

Ghazvini, & Mullis, 2002; Goelmen et al., 2006; Helburn, 1995; Howes & Smith, 1995). Multiple studies have found that toddlers in child care also appear to experience less supportive and sensitive caregiving with harsher and more punitive caregivers than their preschool counterparts (Ghazvini & Mullis, 2002; Kryzer, Kovan, Phillips, Domagall, & Gunnar, 2007; Thomason & La Paro, 2009).

Structural Factors and Their Relationship to Child Care Quality

Research has suggested that structural factors, or factors outside of the child's day-to-day experience, may impact the provision of high-quality care for centers (Bigras et al., 2010; Goelman et al., 2006; Pessanha, Aguiar, & Bairrão, 2007; Raikes, Raikes, & Wilcox, 2005). This study specifically addressed staff turnover and wages as factors associated with quality change. Staff turnover is especially problematic for the quality of care infants and toddlers receive as continuity of care holds significant advantages for this age group. Over time, studies have also found that the remaining caregivers feel additional stress from the process of retraining new hires or picking up the responsibilities of an absent coworker, which can lead to even more turnover (Hale-Jinks, Knopf, & Kemple, 2006; Whitebook & Sakai, 2003). With caregivers feeling more stress, as well as large numbers of untrained or newly trained caregivers, the quality of care is likely to suffer.

While wages are primarily considered a caregiver characteristic, the pervasive low wages in the child care workforce are closely linked with high turnover and thus are discussed in this section (Franko, Brodsky, Wacker, & Estrada, 2017; Whitebook, Howes, & Phillips, 1998; Whitebook & Sakai, 2003; Whitebook, Phillips, & Howes, 2014). The Bureau of Labor Statistics reports the mean hourly wage for "child care workers in the U.S." at $11.42. The Center for the Study of Child Care Employment notes that this wage continues to be lower than animal caregivers (Whitebook et al., 2014). Low wages are repeatedly cited as the cause for teachers and caregivers to leave the workforce if programs can even attract them in the first place (Kovach, 2008; Whitebook & Sakai, 2003). One study found that among 62 participating centers for every unit increase in hourly wage, ITERS scores increased .44 points (St. Clair-Christman, Buell, & Gamel-McCormick, 2011). However, wages alone have not been able to fully explain differences in quality or retention of staff, especially in community based programs (Goelman et al., 2006). This study's findings contribute to a clearer picture of how wages and turnover work together and their relationship with quality in Infant/Toddler (IT) classrooms.

Caregiver Characteristics and the Relationship to Childcare Quality

Poor quality care is also associated with the caregiver workforce. Beyond turnover and wages, caregiver characteristics—such as education, in-service professional development, feelings of professionalism, workplace satisfaction, and supports—play a significant role in the overall quality of a child care program (Helburn, 1995; Ghazvini & Mullis, 2002; Miller & Bogatova, 2009; Phillipsen, Burchinal, Howes, & Cryer, 1997). Several workforce studies have found that infant and toddler caregivers typically receive the least training and are the poorest educated within the early childhood workforce (Dennehy & Marshall, 2005; Gerber et al., 2007; Goelman et al., 2006; Miller & Bogatova, 2009; Whitebook & Sakai, 2003).

In recent years, researchers have explored how formal training and in-service professional development support quality specifically in infant and toddler classrooms. While findings have indicated that formal education, such as college classes and degree obtainment do impact quality, in-service professional development and training also have the potential to significantly impact quality, especially when accompanied with coaching (Burchinal, Cryer, Clifford, & Howes, 2002; Moreno, Green, & Koehn, 2015). Likewise, child outcomes appear to be impacted when quality improvement and in-service training occur concurrently (Egert, Fukkink, & Eckhardt, 2018). Fukkink and Lont (2007) also noted that, like education levels, in-service professional development has had mixed results in terms of the relationship with quality. Some research suggests that the impact of in-service professional development on quality may depend on other variables such as wages, workplace supports, and program auspices (Fuligni, Howes, Lara-Cinisomo, & Karoly, 2009; Torquati, Raikes, & Huddleston-Casas, 2007).

Much of the research on professional development is limited to caregivers at the preschool level and within Head Start programs and does not include infant and toddler caregivers within community child care settings. Zaslow and colleagues highlight that research needs to examine effective strategies for professional development among IT caregivers (Zaslow, Tout, Halle, Whittaker, & Lavelle, 2010). This study specifically addresses the possible relationship between specialized in-service training and quality outcomes by examining whether caregivers who completed a 40-hour Infant and Toddler Endorsement Training were more likely to be in classrooms with higher-quality scores and if other structural variables make a contribution to any existing relationship.

Evaluating Quality Change Efforts

Despite a growing understanding of how structural and caregiver characteristics impact the quality of IT child care, there is still wide debate on how to achieve quality change in programs. Quality improvement initiatives across the country, using varied assessment strategies, have examined a variety of methods for improving quality. Methods typically include mentoring and coaching, in-service training, professional development incentives, and enhancement grants. Not surprisingly, the work has had mixed results (i.e., Fontaine, Torre, Grafwallner, & Underhill, 2006; Weinstock et al., 2012). In a 2005 study, Campbell and Milbourne concluded that training alone is not enough to change quality with less than 8% of classrooms demonstrating observable quality change. In addition, a 2012 evaluation of the widely respected *Program for Infant/Toddler Care (PITC)*, also found no significant changes to program quality. A likely explanation for these findings is high attrition rates among participants.

Training and education, when part of other quality improvement efforts, such as coaching and enhancement grants, do appear to have significant impacts on infant and toddler quality (Brown, Andrews, & Hutchinson, 2008; Egert et al., 2018; Moreno et al., 2015). However, it was noted by Brown and colleagues (2008) that when enhancement grants are a part of quality improvement activities the purchase of new materials or renovation of spaces can have significant impacts on quality scores as measured by the *Infant and Toddler Environmental Rating Scale-Revised* (*ITERS-R*), a common tool for measuring infant and toddler classroom quality, without any change in teacher behavior.

Vandell and Wolfe (2000) hypothesized that quality is the result of varied inputs encompassing regulations, parental income, consumer education, wages, training, and the physical-care environment. They also suggest that a better understanding of the factors that lead to the most quality improvement is needed. While research has identified the factors contributing to quality, the outcomes of quality improvement efforts have been mixed. Few studies have examined how the factors that are associated with high- or low-quality work to effect quality change over time. This study, framed in an ecological perspective, provides further evidence for the factors involved with quality improvement in infants and toddler child care within community-based, private centers and highlights that quality improvement efforts need to address an array of factors if the goal is lasting quality change.

Methods

Sample

This study examined data from 48 centers participating in a statewide *Quality Improvement Project* (QIP) between 2003 and 2010. Centers included 29 operating for profit and 15 nonprofit centers with four centers not reporting a business type. No Early Head Start programs were included though some centers may have had Early Head Start Community Partnership slots. Center capacity ranged from a minimum of 18 children to a maximum of 200 with a mean of 88 ($SD = 46.7$) children. IT capacity (under 24 months) ranged from a minimum of 7 to a maximum of 40 infants and toddlers with a mean of 17 ($SD = 8.6$). Thirty-six centers were located in urban areas; twelve were rural/non-urban. Two centers were accredited by the National Association for the Education of Young Children (NAEYC). All centers were in compliance with state regulations monitoring basic health and safety standards. The data included in this study include classroom level data for all centers participating for 4 years or less.

Measures

Infant and Toddler Environmental Rating Scale-Revised (ITERS-R).
Classroom quality was assessed using the *Infant and Toddler Environmental Rating Scale-Revised* Edition (*ITERS-R*: Harms, Cryer, & Clifford, 2003). The *ITERS-R*, a rigorous, nationally recognized tool, is comprised of the following subscales: Space and Furnishings; Personal Care Routines for Infants and Toddlers; Listening and Talking; Age-appropriate Activities; Adult-Child Interaction; Program Structure including Adult-Child Ratios; and Parent and Staff Communication. Observers rated individual classrooms using a 7-point scale for 39 total items during a 2- to 3-hour observation period. Internal consistency has a Cronbach's alpha = .93 for the complete scale. Reliability checks were completed annually with the project manager and infant/toddler specialists to maintain a minimum of 85% overall reliability.

Results

Descriptive Statistics

Participation rates. Participation dropped drastically across the 7 years of the study period with 86 classrooms within 48 centers participating at the baseline assessment and receiving at least one post-treatment assessment. The second post treatment assessment was completed with 71 classrooms. By the third post-treatment assessment over 60% ($n = 52$) of the original sample had dropped from participation, meaning that the center and/or classrooms did not participate in the QIP for more than 3 years. In year 7 of the QIP only five classrooms remained participating and just over 94% ($n = 81$) of the original 86 classrooms had dropped.

Infant and Toddler Endorsement (ITE) One component of the QIP program was the mandate that administration and teaching staff complete 40 hours of IT training and obtain their ITE. Table 1 describes the percentage of classrooms that reported at least one teacher working on their ITE and the percentage of classrooms reporting at least one teacher with a completed ITE.

Wages, Turnover, and Parent Fees. Three variables of interest to this research included average wages of teachers, turnover rates of teachers, and the rates for care. Table 2 summarizes the means for each of these variables over the 7-year study period. A turnover rate (percent) for each classroom was calculated by taking the total number of teachers who had left from one year to the next and dividing it by the total number of teachers within the same time period.

ITERS-R Scores. Also described in Table 2 are the means and standard deviations for total *ITERS-R* Scores. A paired sample t-test revealed a significant increase in *ITERS-R* scores between T1 and T2 ($t = -3.146$, $df = 60$, $p = .003$) and a significant decrease in mean scores between T3 and T4 ($t = 2.8$, $df = 30$, $p = .009$). Statistically significant change among *ITERS-R* scores can occur with very little actual point change. The change in score from T1 to T2 also represents an observable change in that the mean of the centers moved from the "minimal" range of quality to the "good" range.

Table 1
Infant and Toddler Endorsement (ITE) by Classroom

	T0 N(77)	T1 N(80)	T2 N(63)	T3 N(33)	T4 N(23)	T5 N(14)
Classrooms with > 0 teachers working on endorsement	22%	35%	35%	15%	33%	35%
Classrooms with > 0 teachers completed endorsement	25%	51%	63%	66%	56%	57%

Correlations

Correlations were calculated at each time point from baseline (T0) through T4 to identify existing relationships between *ITERS-R* scores and the independent variables of wages, turnover rates, and number of teachers with a completed ITE. Due to the highly correlated nature of the *ITERS-R* subscales with the total average *ITERS-R* score (r ranging from .82 to .91, $p < .001$), correlations are only reported for the total average score. Correlations are reported in Tables 3 through 6. A significant relationship between *ITERS-R* average scores, turnover, and the number of teachers with ITE is significant at T1 and continues to be significant through T4. At T3 and T4 wages also appeared to be significantly linked.

Mixed Models

A mixed model analysis was used to explore the relationship of independent variables with *ITERS-R* scores over time (Seltman, 2012; Shek & Ma, 2011). The mixed model analysis had three benefits for exploring how the variables of interest impacted quality change. First, the mixed model approach accounts for the possible violation of independent observations inherent in the repeated use of the *ITERS-R* within and between centers and across years. Secondly, a mixed model is able to handle the unequal sample sizes and missing data as centers stopped participating in the QIP at different time

Table 2
Means and Standard Deviations for Wages, Turnover, Parent Fees and ITERS-R Scores Over Time

Variable	T0 Mean	SD	T1 Mean	SD	T2 Mean	SD	T3 Mean	SD	T4 Mean	SD	T5 Mean	SD	T6 Mean	SD
Hourly Wage	$7.60 N(74)	$1.46	$7.75 N(70)	$1.33	$8.73 N(41)	$1.78	$7.80 N(33)	$2.08	$7.87 N(23)	$1.30	$7.79 N(13)	$1.19	$7.97 N(3)	$0.47
Turnover	50% N(83)		71% N(63)		56% N(32)		60% N(32)		62% N(24)		46% N(14)		70% N(5)	
					37%		41%		40%		43%		45%	
Rates	$557.00 N(77)	$127.55	$590.08 N(60)	$122.36	$588.71 N(32)	$84.81	$593.00 N(21)	$124.70	$597.20 N(17)	$82.41	$658.41 N(14)	$85.28	$652.00 N(5)	$57.18
Total ITERS-R	3.8	1.2	3.8	0.9	4.2	0.8	3.8	0.9	3.9	0.1	3.6	0.6	4.1	0.2

Table 3
Correlations Between Variables at Treatment Time 1 (T1)

Variable	Average ITERS-R scores	Wages	# of teachers with endorsement	Rate for classroom	Turnover	Gain/no gain
Average ITERS-R score		-.00	.25*	-.15	-.23*	-.23*
Wages			.04	.61**	.05	-.22
# of teachers with endorsement				.06	-.40**	-.09
Rate for classroom					.15	-.35**
Turnover						-.10

*p < .05, **p < .01, ***p < .001.

Table 4
Correlations Between Variables at Treatment Time 2 (T2)

Variable	Average ITERS-R scores	Wages	# of teachers with endorsement	Rate for classroom	Turnover	Gain/no gain
Average ITERS-R score		.16	.21	.04	-.13	-.31*
Wages			.03	.23	-.10	.16
# of teachers with endorsement				-.28	-.37**	.09
Rate for classroom					.08	.04
Turnover						-.02

*p < .05, **p < .01, ***p < .001.

Table 5
Correlations Between Variables at Treatment Time 3 (T3)

Variable	Average ITERS-R scores	Wages	# of teachers with endorsement	Rate for classroom	Turnover	Gain/no gain
Average ITERS-R score		.10	.25	.19	-.38*	.65**
Wages			.45**	.11	-.10	-.01
# of teachers with endorsement				-.14	-.52**	-.02
Rate for classroom					.19	.20
Turnover						-.04

*p < .05, **p < .01, ***p < .001.

Table 6
Correlations Between Variables at Treatment Time 4 (T4)

Variable	Average ITERS-R scores	Wages	# of teachers with endorsement	Rate for classroom	Turnover	Gain/no gain
Average ITERS-R score		.51*	.04	-.02	-.18	.38
Wages			.54*	.19	-.34	.08
# of teachers with endorsement				-.05	-.49*	-.19
Rate for classroom					-.02	-.14
Turnover						.08

*p < .05, **p < .01, ***p < .001.

points. Lastly, the mixed model was able to assess for variance among the group mean and individual variance for the classrooms nested within centers. Due to the small sample size and highly correlated nature of variables, one model was developed for each variable of interest to examine how that variable impacted *ITERS-R* scores. The first model addressed only the role of time on *ITERS-R* scores. Only the *ITERS-R* total average score was used as the dependent variable. The mixed model form of , where is the vector of the *ITERS-R* scores, represents the fixed effects for variable one to the nth variable, is the vector of the fixed effect parameters, and is the vector of residual errors was applied (SPSS Technical Report, 2002). All variables were considered to have fixed effects.

Model 1 was comprised of *ITERS-R* scores and treatment time to assess if classroom average *ITERS-R* scores increased over subsequent years of participation (up to 6 years after baseline). Model 1 indicates that there were no significant differences in *ITERS-R* scores across treatment times (β ranged from .27 to -.40 at T5, p ranging from .45 to .33). In fact, *ITERS-R* scores appeared to decrease slightly, though not significantly, for those centers who participated in the QIP the longest ($\beta = -.40$, $SE = .40$, $p = .33$). However, this is contrary to the results of the paired sample t-test reported above that did find a significant increase in average *ITERS-R* scores from T1 to T2. Unlike the paired sample t-test, which excluded cases with missing values, the mixed model allows cases with missing values and is more sensitive to mean changes, which may explain the difference in results. To examine if the results of the paired sample t-test could be replicated using the mixed model analysis, Model 2 was created by reverse coding treatment time and only included baseline, T1, T2, T3, and T4 due to the drastic sample size decrease at T5. Results of Model 2 did find significant increases in *ITERS-R* scores at T2 compared to T1 or baseline ($\beta = .35$, $SE = .13$, $p = .007$). Beyond T2 changes in the *ITERS-R* scores were still not significant.

Mixed-model analyses were run with the independent variables each being placed in their own model. Model 3 used *ITERS-R* scores as the dependent variable and number of teachers who had completed the ITE as the differing variable with time as the repeated measure and included baseline through T4. The continuous variable of number of teachers with ITE was recoded into two levels, classrooms with zero teachers completed and those with one or more teachers completed (three teachers being the most any one classroom had). The results of model 3 indicate that classrooms with zero teachers having completed the ITE had on average a .33 decrease in their ITERS-R score ($\beta = -.33$, $SE = .12$, $p = .007$).

Model 4 examined how turnover impacted *ITERS-R* scores over time. The continuous variable of turnover was also recoded into four levels (0 to 25% $n = 53$; 26 to 50% $n = 58$; 51 to 75% $n = 17$; and 76% or higher $n = 95$ (*N*'s are based on all classrooms over time) based on quartiles. Classrooms with the lowest levels of teacher turnover (between zero and 25%) have significantly higher scores than those with the highest level of turnover ($\beta = .40$, $SE = .15$, $p = .008$). Turnover was reexamined at two levels by splitting the sample into those classrooms who had between zero and 50-percent turnover ($N = 111$ classrooms from Baseline to T6) and those that had 51% or more turnover ($N = 112$ classrooms from Baseline to T6). Results were similar to the quartile breakdown of turnover with classrooms experiencing 50% or less turnover more likely to have significantly higher scores on their *ITERS-R* average over time than those with greater turnover ($\beta = .34$, $SE = .12$, $p = .005$).

Other models that included geographic location (urban versus non-urban), parent fees, and wages were found to be insignificant in impacting *ITERS-R* scores over time in this sample.

Discussion

Quality improvement initiatives, like the QIP, continue to be a primary method for states and communities to assist programs with raising the quality of care, though results from these projects remain mixed. With limited funding for infant and toddler child care, it is important for states to have a clear understanding of the factors related to quality change to better capitalize on what works to increase quality, improve child outcomes, and efficiently use limited public funding in community-based programs.

Similar to other evaluations of quality improvement initiatives (Uttley & Horm, 2008; Weinstock et al., 2012), findings from this study suggest that actual quality improvement is minimal across time when examining average *ITERS-R* scores. However, this result may oversimplify the issue as those programs that completed the training component did experience quality increases.

The paired sample t-test and Model 2 of the mixed analysis reveal that there was a statistically significant increase from T1 to T2 for mean *ITERS-R* scores. However, after T2 mean scores did not continue to increase and even decreased for those centers participating the longest (though not significantly). These findings indicate that short-term (1 year or less) interventions may not provide enough time for programs to make changes but long term programs (extending over multiple years) are also not effective. Results from this sample suggest that 2 years of intervention allowed enough time for programs to make changes that increase quality but not allowing so much time that programs became complacent. Currently many QRIS systems reward programs that continue to maintain quality, and while it is important to continue investing in those programs working to provide high quality, funding alone may not lead to continuous quality improvement.

Training

While several factors did not appear to significantly impact *ITERS-R* scores, Model 3 of the mixed model analysis indicates that having at least one teacher in a classroom with an ITE contributed significantly to higher *ITERS-R* scores. However, the percentage of classrooms that had at least one teacher with the ITE never exceeded 66% (T3). Those working on the ITE (having completed at least 10 hours of the 40-hour course) never exceeded 35%. Relatively low numbers of ITEs were observed despite the QIP requirement that at least one teacher per classroom should obtain the ITE. High-turnover rates may provide an explanation for the lack of teachers with ITEs. Teachers may not stay long enough in one classroom to complete the 40 hours of training. However, the lack of participation in the IT training, especially in light of its significant effect on increasing quality, is concerning. Zaslow et al. (2010) recognized that, to date, little research on professional development among IT caregivers had been conducted. This finding has significant implications for the field in terms of the importance of specific IT in-service training and its resulting impact on classroom quality. Much of the literature shows mixed results for the impact of professional development on quality, but the finding in this research that the ITE is related to higher quality supports Fukkink and Lont's (2007) assertion that specialized and age-specific programs are likely more effective than universally administered programs that do not focus on the unique developmental needs of a given age group. If specialized training can improve IT classroom quality, this may be an attainable and cost effective route to obtaining higher quality but only if turnover can be controlled.

Turnover

High teacher turnover has long been recognized as problematic for the early care and education field and is linked to poor quality (Cryer, Hurwitz, & Wolery, 2000; Helburn, 1995; Whitebook et al., 1998). Mean turnover for this sample across the study period was 57%, with many programs experiencing 100% turnover multiple times. Findings from this study continue to support the assertion that high turnover and low quality are inextricably linked. Often the relationship between turnover and low quality is explained through low wages. However, this study did not find wages playing a significant role in either turnover or quality. Qualitative data collected from 10 center directors participating in the QIP indicated that turnover may be more linked to center culture and leadership practices, a finding echoed in business management and nursing fields (Cummings et al., 2018; Waldman, Carter, & Hom, 2015).

Turnover and number of teachers with an ITE were highly negatively correlated. This provides an additional explanation for why the ITE leads to higher quality. Completing the 40 hours of training and putting into practice gained skills and knowledge takes time. As stated above, the classrooms that had higher turnover may not have had teachers who stayed long enough to complete the training; thus they were at a disadvantage not only due to the high turnover and lack of continuity but also because their teachers are not gaining the necessary skills and knowledge to address classroom quality.

These findings have significant implications for the field as quality improvement projects typically provide a universal program of training, grants, and coaching, but neglect to focus on individual program needs. To see the best results in quality improvement, initiatives should begin by assessing at the onset a variety of factors, including personal characteristics, turnover rates, workplace environment, and director perceptions and then develop with the director a target approach to best meet the program's individual needs.

Limitations

Similar to other non-experimental design studies, this study presents a number of limitations including high attrition, selection bias, and the inclusion of self-reported data. In addition, while protocols were in place to maintain inter-rater reliability, raters were also coaches in the program and thus may present unintended bias within their ratings. It should also be noted that implementation fidelity of the QIP was not assessed in this research study. Conclusions about the efficacy of the project are limited and should be taken cautiously as this study does not address the consistent implementation of training.

Implications

Despite the limitation of this study, the results carry important implications for understanding quality change within infant and toddler classrooms in community-based child care centers. Community-based programs rely on tuition from families to operate their programs, with costs for supporting high-quality care often exceeding what families can afford to pay and thus shifting the burden from consumers to the workforce (Franko et al., 2017). Meanwhile, the recognition of the importance of high quality environments for infants and toddlers has increased leading to increased state regulations and requirements within Quality Rating and Improvement Systems. Likewise, the demand for infant and toddler child care also continues to rise as families with all available adults in the workforce become the norm. Despite increasing demands for quality and increasing need wages for community-based early-childhood teachers has barely increased in over 25 years (Whitebook et al., 2014). The challenge for policy makers and practitioners is developing systems that invest in sustained quality change, especially in infant and toddler classrooms, while addressing the underlying challenges of turnover that result from poor compensation, job satisfaction, and workplace culture.

Results from this study suggest that specific training for teachers in infant and toddler care and development is a valuable factor for obtaining higher quality. Specific training may also help to decrease turnover as teachers who feel more competent in their work may be less likely to experience burnout. However, it is important to note that a recent survey of the early childhood workforce found additional in-service professional development to be desired but often out of reach for many professionals due to the cost of attending or the need to take time off to attend (Shaack & Le, 2017). Few low-paying jobs in the United States require employees to obtain additional training or college classes without funding both the time to take the class and the cost of the class. However, the traditional funding models prevalent in private, community-based centers often place this burden squarely on the shoulders of the teacher or caregiver. State policy makers and foundations should consider increasing investments in supporting in-service infant and toddler teachers to obtain specialized training. However, much of the literature is in agreement that training alone cannot increase quality and must be coupled with coaching and enhancement funding for space and materials (Brown et al., 2008; Moreno et al., 2014).

This study also reinforces that professional development resulting in actual increases to quality is further complicated by high turnover rates pervasive within the workforce. Turnover appears to present a significant barrier to quality with direct implications for child outcomes High turnover is often the result of a combination of low job satisfaction, wages, and workplace culture within community-based centers (Hale-Jinks et al., 2006). While state quality rating and improvement systems have built in incentives for programs to retain staff and increase wages, it is often not realistic for community programs to do these things and thus change needs to occur at both the policy level and at the practice level for programs. Further research is needed into policies and practices that are cost effective in supporting lower turnover within programs, especially among infant and toddler teachers. In addition, consumer awareness focusing on the value of quality infant/toddler care on child outcomes and the economic stability of communities needs to drive policy change to increase outside funding to community-based child care programs providing teachers with the professional respect their valuable job deserves.

References

Bigras, N., Bouchard, C., Cantin, G., Brunson, L., Coutu, S., Lemay, L., . . . Charron, A. (2010). A comparative study of structural and process quality in center-based and family-based child care services. *Child Youth Care Forum, 39*, 129–150. doi:10.1007/s10566-009-9088-4

Brown, E., Andrews, A.B., & Hutchison, L. (2008). Bridging the quality gap: Increasing the environmental quality of small independent rural infant-toddler child care. *Early Childhood Services, 2*(2), 89–110.

Burchinal, M.R., Cryer, D., Clifford, R.M., & Howes, C. (2002). Caregiver training and classroom quality in child care centers. *Applied Developmental Science, 6*(1), 2-11. doi:10.1207/S1532480XADS0601_01

Burchinal, M.R., Roberts, J.E., Nabors, L.A., & Bryant, D.M. (1996). Quality of center child care and infant cognitive and language development. *Child Development, 67*(2), 606-620. Retrieved from http://www.jstor.org/stable/1131835

Campbell, P.H., & Millbourne, S.A. (2005). Improving the quality of infant-toddler care through professional development. *Topics in Early Childhood Special Education, 25*(1), 3-14. doi:10.1177/02711214050250010101

Cryer, D., Hurwitz, S., & Wolery, M. (2000). Continuity of caregiver for infants and toddlers in center-based child care: Report on a survey of center practices. *Early Childhood Research Quarterly, 15*(4), 497-514. doi:10.1016/S0885-2006(01)00069-2

Cummings, G.G., Tate, K., Lee, S., Wong, C.A., Paananen, T., Micaroni, S.P.M., & Chattejee, G.E. (2018). Leadership styles and outcome patterns for the nursing workforce and work environment: A systemic review. *International Journal of Nursing Studies, 85,* 19-60. doi:10.1016/jinnurstu.2018.04.016

Dennehy, J., & Marhsall, N.L. (2005). *Workforce characteristics of infant and toddler caregivers in centers, family child care homes, and Early Head Start programs: A Massachusetts capacity study research brief.* Wellesley, MA: Center for Research on Women.

Egert, F., Fukkink, R.G., & Eckhardt, A.G. (2018). Impact of in-service professional development programs for early childhood teachers on quality ratings and child outcomes: A meta-anlysis. *Review of Education Research, 88*(3), 401-433. doi:10.3102/0034654317751918.

Fontaine, N.S., Torre, L.D., Grafwallner, R., & Underhill, B. (2006). Increasing quality in early care and learning environments. *Early Child Development and Care, 176*(2), 157-169. doi:10.1080/0300443042000302690

Franko. M., Brodsky, A., Wacker, A., & Estrada, M. (2017). *Bearing the cost of early care and education in Colorado: An economic analysis.* Denver, CO: Butler Institute for Families, Graduate School of Social Work, University of Denver.

Fukkink, R.G., & Lont, A. (2007). Does training matter? A meta-analysis and review of caregiver training studies. *Early Childhood Research Quarterly, 22,* 294-311. doi:10.1016/j.ecresq.2007.04.005

Fuligni, A.S., Howes, C., Lara-Cinisomo, S., & Karoly, L. (2009). Diverse pathways in early childhood professional development: An exploration of early educators in public preschools, private preschools, and family child care homes. *Early Education & Development, 20*(3), 507-526. doi:10.1080/10409280902783483

Gerber, E.B., Whitebook, M., & Weinstein, R.S. (2007). At the heart of child care: Predictors of teacher sensitivity in center-based child care. *Early Childhood Research Quarterly, 22,* 327–346. doi:10.101/j.ecresq.2006.12.003

Ghazvini, A., & Mullis, R.L. (2002). Center-based care for young children: Examining predictors of quality. *The Journal of Genetic Psychology, 163*(1), 112–125. doi: 10.1080/00221320209597972

Goelman, H., Forer, B., Kershaw, P., Doherty, G., Lero, D., & LaGrange, A. (2006). Towards a predictive model of quality in Canadian child care centers. *Early Childhood Research Quarterly, 21,* 280–295. doi:10.1016/j.ecresq.2006.07.005

Hale-Jinks, C., Knopf, H., & Kemple, K. (2006). Tackling teacher turnover in child care: Understanding the causes and consequences, identifying solutions. *Childhood Education, 82*(4), 219–226. doi:10.1080/00094056.2006.10522826

Harms, T., Cryer, D., & Clifford, R. (2003). *Infant/Toddler Environmental Rating Scale.* New York, NY: Teachers College Press.

Helburn, S.W. (1995). *Cost, quality and child outcomes in child care centers. Technical Report, Public Report, and Executive Summary.* Denver, CO: University of Colorado.

Howes, C., & Smith, E.W. (1995). Relations among child care quality, teacher behavior, children's play activities, emotional security, and cognitive play. *Early Childhood Research Quarterly, 10,* 381–404. doi:10.1016/0885-2006(95)900

Kovach, M. (2008). Child care provider survey reveals cost constrains quality. *Research Brief, 96*(5).

Kryzer, E.M., Kovan, N., Phillips, D.A., Domagall, L.A., & Gunnar, M.R. (2007). Toddlers' and preschoolers' experience in family day care: Age differences and behavioral correlates. *Early Childhood Research Quarterly, 22*(4), 451–466. doi:10.1016/j.ecresq.2007.08.004

Miller, J.A., & Bogatova, T. (2009). Quality improvements in the early care and education workforce: Outcomes and impact of the T.E.A.C.H. Early Childhood project. *Evaluation and Program Planning, 32,* 257–277. doi:10.1016/j.evalprogplan.2009.02.001

Moreno, A.J., Green, S., & Koehn, J. (2015). The effectiveness of coursework and coaching at improving quality of care in infant-toddler settings. *Early Education and Development, 26,* 66–88. doi:10.1080/10409289.2014.941260

Pessanha, M., Aguiar, C., & Bairrão, J. (2007). Influence of structural features on Portuguese toddler child care quality. *Early Childhood Research Quarterly, 22,* 204–214. doi:10.1016/j.ecresq.2007.02.003

Phillipsen, L.C., Burchinal, M.R., Howes, C., & Cryer, D. (1997). The prediction of process quality from structural features of child care. *Early Childhood Research Quarterly, 12*, 281–303. doi:10.1016/S0885-2006(97)90004-1

Raikes, H.A., Raikes, H.H., & Wilcox, B. (2005). Regulation, subsidy receipt and provider characteristics: What predicts quality in child care homes? *Early Childhood Research Quarterly, 20*, 164–184. doi:10.1016/j.ecresq.2005.04.006

Seltman, H.J. (2012). *Experimental design and analysis*. Retrieved from http://www.stat.cmu.edu/~hseltman/309/Book/Book.pdf

Shaack, D. D. & Le, V. (2017). *Supporting the educational attainment and professional development needs of Colorado's early educator workforce (Research Brief #2)*. Denver, CO: Early Milestones Colorado. Retrieved from http://earlymilestones.org/wp-content/uploads/2017/09/Brief_2_CO_EC_Workforce_Survey.pdf

Shek, D.T.L., & Ma, C.M.S. (2011). Longitudinal data analyses using linear mixed models in SPSS: Concepts, procedures and illustrations. *The Scientific World Journal, 11*, 42–76. doi:10.1100/tsw.2011.2

SPSS Technical Report. (2002). *Linear mixed-effects modeling in SPSS: An introduction to the mixed procedure*. Retrieved from http://www.spss.ch/upload/1126184451_Linear%20Mixed%20Effects%20Modeling%20in%20SPSS.pdf

St.Clair-Christman, J.M., Buell, M., & Gamel-McCormick, M. (2011). Money matters for early education: The relationship among child care quality, teacher characteristics, and subsidy status. *Early Childhood Research and Practice, 13*(2). Retrieved from http://ecrp.uiuc.edu/v13n2/christman.html

Thomason, A.C., & La Paro, K.M. (2009). Measuring the quality of teacher-child interactions in toddler child care. *Early Education and Development, 20*(2), 285–304. doi:10.1080/10409280902773351

Torquati, J.C., Raikes, H., & Huddleston-Casas, C.A. (2007). Teacher education, motivation, compensation, workplace support, and links to quality of center-based child care and teachers' intention to stay in the early childhood profession. *Early Childhood Research Quarterly, 22*, 261–275. doi: 10.1016/j.ecresq.2007.03.004

Uttley, C.M., & Horm, D.M. (2008). Mentoring in early childhood professional development: Evaluation of the Rhode Island Child Development Specialist Apprenticeship Program. *Journal of Early Childhood Teacher Education, 29*(3), 237–252. doi:10.1080/10901020802275286

Vandell, D.L., & Wolfe, B. (2000). *Child care quality: Does it matter and does it need to be improved? (Report No 78)*. Madison, WI: Institute for Research on Poverty.

Waldman, D.A., Carter, M.Z., & Hom, P.W. (2015). A multilevel investigation of leadership and turnover behavior. *Journal of Management, 41*(6), 1724–1744. doi:10.1177/0149206312460679

Weinstock, P., Bos, J., Tseng, F., Rosenthal, E., Ortiz, L., Dowsett, C., & Bentley, A. (2012). *Evaluation of Program for Infant/Toddler Care (PITC): An on-site training of caregivers* (NCEE 2012-4003). Washington, DC: National Center for Education Evaluation and Regional Assistance, U.S. Department of Education. Retrieved from http://0ies.ed.gov.opac.acc.msmc.edu/ncee/edlabs/regions/west/pdf/REL_20124003.pdf

Whitebook, M., Howes, C., & Phillips, D. (1998). *Worthy work, unlivable wages: The National Child Care Staffing Study, 1988–1997*. Washington, DC: Center for the Child Care Workforce.

Whitebook, M., Phillips, D., & Howes, C. (2014). *Worthy work, still unlivable wages: The early childhood workforce 25 years after the National Child Care Staffing Study*. Berkeley, CA: Center for the Study of Child Care Employment, University of California, Berkeley.

Whitebook, M., & Sakai, L. (2003). Turnover begets turnover: Examination of job and occupational instability among child care center staff. *Early Childhood Research Quarterly, 18*, 273–293. doi:10.1016/S0885-2006(03)00040-1

Zaslow, M., Tout, K., Halle, T., Whittaker, J.V., & Lavelle, B. (2010). *Toward the identification of features of effective professional development for early childhood educators: A literature review*. Bethesda, MD: Child Trends.

Exploring Culture, Race, and Ethnicity in Early Childhood Mental Health Consultation: The Role of the Consultative Alliance

Anna E. Davis, Eva Marie Shivers, and Deborah F. Perry

Abstract

Young boys of color are at disproportionate risk for suspension and expulsion from child care indicating that race and culture may influence disciplinary decisions. It is therefore necessary to investigate efforts to mitigate expulsion risk as well as the potential role of race and culture in these efforts. Early Childhood Mental Health Consultation (ECMHC) has been shown to be associated with reduced rates of expulsion. Prior research indicates that the positive effects of ECMHC are influenced by a strong positive relationship between a consultant and an educator—a construct referred to by Davis (2018) as the Consultative Alliance (CA). The current study sought to expand upon these findings to assess whether variables related to race and culture affected the CA, ECMHC outcomes, and/or the link between the two. Participants were young children ($n = 316$, average age = 42 months), early educators ($n = 289$) and MHCs ($n = 62$) from child care centers in a southwestern state. Results of moderation analyses conducted within multilevel models indicated that, for some outcomes, the predictive power of CA was stronger when the focus child for mental health consultation was a boy of color, the consultant had self-reported expertise in cultural diversity, and the educator and consultant were racially/ethnically matched. Taken together, these results suggest that adding a cultural lens to our exploration of the effectiveness of ECMHC may enhance our understanding of how racial disparities in child care programs might be mitigated.

***Keywords*: early childhood mental health consultation, consultative alliance, racial equity, early childhood education**

Early childhood education (ECE) is grounded in the ideal that all young children deserve access to equal, high-quality early learning opportunities to prepare them to succeed in school (Magnuson & Shager, 2010). While there has been marked progress in this effort in recent decades, there are still disparities based on race and gender with regard to children's experiences in early care and education settings as well as access to quality child care. For instance, African American children are least likely to be enrolled in ECE programs that are considered high quality (Barnett, Carolan, & Johns, 2013) and are rated lower on their school readiness at age four (Barbarin, 2007; Reardon & Portilla, 2016).

One of the most glaring examples of disparities in early care and education settings is in exclusionary discipline (suspensions and expulsions). Research to date has demonstrated that children of color experience harsher discipline for the same behaviors as their White peers (Kirwan Institute, 2015; Raible & Irizarry, 2010). Specifically, African American and Latino boys in preschool have disproportionally higher rates of expulsion than their same age White and Asian peers (Gilliam, 2005; U.S. Department of Education, Office of Civil Rights, 2016). Of note, consistent with recent publications, the terms "children of color" and "boys of color" will be used in this article to describe ethnic minority youth in a way that is inclusive of a wide range of cultural and ethnic backgrounds (Barbarin, Murry, Tolan, & Graham, 2016; My Brother's Keeper Task Force, 2016).

When children experience harsh disciplinary practices, they are at risk for further and, perhaps, compounding negative developmental outcomes. Expulsion may exacerbate early academic and social-emotional disparities and predict disengagement from school, diminished educational opportunity, and eventual dropout—all of which may increase the risk for unemployment and lack of economic self-sufficiency (American Academy of Pediatrics, 2013; American Psychological Association Zero Tolerance Task Force, 2008; U.S. Department of Health and Human Services and the U.S. Department of Education, 2014).

Researchers have identified some the following drivers of child care suspension and expulsion: low program quality, inadequate knowledge of child development, racial discipline disparities, and early childhood trauma (Meek & Gilliam, 2016; McCann, Shivers, & Means, 2018). Some scholars and policy makers hypothesize that implicit and explicit bias are some of the mechanisms leading to these discipline disparities (Adamu & Hogan, 2015; Okonofua & Eberhardt, 2015; U.S. Department of Health and Human Services and U.S. Department of Education, 2014). Other factors that may contribute to preschool discipline disparities include: cultural mismatches between educators and children, low expectations based on deeply rooted racial socialization history in the United States, and misguided preparation for a world filled with bias (Adamu & Hogan, 2015; Gilliam, Maupin, Reyes, Accavitti, & Shic, 2016; Tenenbaum & Ruck, 2007; U.S. Department of Health and Human Services and U.S. Department of Education, 2014).

Early Childhood Mental Health Consultation (ECMHC) is an approach shown to predict reductions in rates of expulsions from child care (Gilliam, 2005; Hepburn, Perry, Shivers, & Gilliam, 2013). In the first national study of preschool expulsion, researchers found that expulsions were significantly lower when there was an early childhood mental health consultant present (Gilliam, 2005). In ECMHC, mental health consultants (MHCs) work within childcare centers (as well as licensed family child care settings) to build staff capacity to address challenging behaviors and promote a healthy social-emotional climate (Cohen & Kaufmann, 2000; 2005; Substance Abuse Mental Health Services Administration, 2014). While each case is tailored to the needs of the educator and center, MHCs typically consult individually with educators to align goals, discuss strategies, provide empathy and validation, and create space for self-reflection (Hunter, Davis, Perry, & Jones, 2016; Johnston & Brinamen, 2012). In addition to reduced expulsion, other positive impacts of ECMHC include improved educator-child relationships, decreased externalizing behavior, and reduced educator stress (Gilliam, Maupin, & Reyes, 2016; Hepburn et al., 2013).

Given the existing research quantifying the overall positive impacts of ECMHC, it is important to move beyond the main effects and expose moderators that may attenuate or enhance these outcomes. The Harvard Center for the Developing Child, Frontiers of Innovation initiative emphasizes the importance of a strong theory of change, well-articulated targets and outcomes, and explicit tests of variables that may moderate the main effects of an intervention on outcomes (Harvard University Center on the Developing Child, 2018). In terms of a theory of change, there is theoretical and empirical support for the idea that the MHC-educator relationship may be an important mechanism of change in ECMHC. This relationship, termed the "Consultative Alliance (CA)" by Davis (2018), reflects the extent to which the educator and MHC perceive that they are partners in the work of consultation, and includes the warmth and positive emotional tone of their interactions. Stronger CA is thought to be facilitated by consistency in availability, mutually agreed upon goals and plans, perspective-taking, clear communication, respect for the unique culture of each child care center, and willingness to explore potentially difficult topics (Green, Everhart, Gordon, & Gettman, 2006; Johnston & Brinamen, 2006; Sheridan, Rispoli, & Holmes, 2014).

In preliminary studies, CA has been shown to have a main effect on teacher perceptions of consultation's impact, educator-child closeness, child attachment behaviors, classroom climate, educator self-efficacy, and educator job resources (Davis, 2018; Green et al., 2006). Moving beyond main effects, it is not yet known for whom this mechanism of change is most impactful. Importantly, there is some indication that ECMHC may have a larger positive effect for the educators of African American and Latino boys than for educators of their White peers (Shivers, Farago, Guimond, & Steier, manuscript in preparation). It is therefore possible that the stronger impact for boys of color relates to the role of the CA in the consultation process. Given the critical role of race and culture in child care settings, disciplinary decisions, and ECMHC, this study sought to explore potential interconnections among CA, race/culture, and various ECMHC outcomes to refine our understanding of how and for whom mental health consultation works and whether it is working for young boys of color. Specifically, this study investigated the following questions: 1) Do race and culture variables, including child race/ethnicity, MHC's self-reported expertise in cultural diversity, and MHC-educator racial/ethnic match, predict the strength of the CA? 2) Do outcomes of ECMHC depend upon these same race/cultural variables? and 3) Does the strength of the link between CA and positive ECMHC outcomes depend upon these same variables? The race/cultural variables were chosen because of their relevance for early childhood educational policy and practice, and as targets for future refinements of a culturally responsive ECMHC approach.

Methods

Participants

Participants were children ($n = 316$), educators ($n = 289$), and MHCs ($n = 62$) who engaged in Early Childhood Mental Health Consultation (ECMHC) in a southwestern state between 2010 and 2014. The data were nested, such that MHCs worked with multiple educators ($M = 8.11$ educators, $SD = 6.89$, range = 1-36), and educators reported on one (90.7%) or two (9.3%) focus children. The average child age was 42 months ($SD = 12$ months, range = 5-73 months). Approximately half of the children were White (54.5%) and approximately three-quarters (73.6%) were boys. The other races/ethnicities in the sample included Latino (22.8%) and African American (12.5%). Less than one in ten (7.3%) had a diagnosed disability.

Educators' racial/ethnic backgrounds roughly paralleled the children's. Almost all educators were female (98.3%), and their ages and levels of education were variable. MHCs were also mostly female (93.5%), and they were more likely to be White (74.2%) and to have a Master's degree (95.2%). Educators and MHCs worked in licensed child care centers, approximately half of which served low-income communities or a combination of low- and middle-income communities (59.6%). Additional information about educator and MHC demographics can be found in Table 1.

Procedures

These data were gathered as part of the longitudinal program evaluation for a statewide system of ECMHC, which was provided free of charge upon request from centers. Consultation was programmatic, classroom-focused, child-focused, or some combination of the three. MHCs' work was tailored to each center, but typically included classroom observations, individual meetings with educators, staff trainings, meetings with families, and consultations with center directors. Some centers were also served concurrently by other quality improvement staff.

Respondents provided data at baseline and 6 months. While additional data were collected at 12 and 18 months, these data were excluded from analyses given high levels of missing data. Missing data mostly reflected the challenge of maintaining the same educator-child dyad in the program because children move classrooms often. The full report of the program's impact and effectiveness was completed by Shivers (2015).

Measures

Consultative alliance. To measure CA, a single item from the 6-month MHC satisfaction survey was used. The item asked MHCs to rate the "Quality of their relationship with this educator" from 1 (low) to 10 (high). The item was log-transformed to correct for skew. This is a common statistical procedure for non-normal distributions (McDonald, 2014). Educator perspectives on the relationship could not be included in analyses because they were so negatively skewed (i.e., scores were consistently high such that there was a ceiling effect) that they could not be corrected by data transformations.

Classroom climate. The Preschool Mental Health Climate Scale (PMHCS; Gilliam, 2008) was designed to assess the aspects of the classroom climate targeted in ECMHC. It is an observational measure that was completed by MHCs. Items are rated on a 5-point Likert scale from "Never/Not True" to "Consistently/Completely True." Observations are summarized into subscales for Positive Indicators (50 items) and Negative Indicators (9 items). Positive Indicators include positive educator-child interaction, cooperation among staff, and support for classroom transitions. Negative Indicators include harsh discipline and over-stimulating physical environments. Pilot data indicated that there was solid internal consistency (Cronbach's alpha = 0.75-0.98) and inter-rater reliability (Cohen's Kappa = 0.71-0.75) for each subscale.

Student-educator relationship. The Student-Teacher Relationship Scale-Short Form (STRS-SF; Pianta, 2001) is a 15-item educator-report scale. Educators reported the extent to which each statement applied to their relationship with a specific child on a 5-point Likert scale. This scale has two subscales: Closeness and Conflict, each with acceptable psychometric properties (Cronbach's alphas α = .86, .92; test-retest reliability r = .88, .92; Pianta, 2001).

Educator self-efficacy. The Teacher Opinion Survey, Revised (TOS) was used to measure educators' self-efficacy and hopelessness (Geller & Lynch, 1999). Educators rated the extent to which they agreed with statements about themselves on a 5-point Likert scale. The Self-Efficacy subscale captured educator perceptions that they were capable of making a difference for children, while the Hopeless/Overwhelmed subscale captured the extent to which educators felt that child outcomes were "out of their hands."

Child resilience factors. The Devereux Early Childhood Assessment (DECA; LeBuffe & Naglierie, 1999; 2003; Mackrain & LeBuffe, 2007) is an educator-report measure of child protective factors. Educators rate on a 5-point Likert scale the frequency of a series of child behaviors over the span of the past 4 weeks. The three subscales are Attachment, Initiative, and Self-Control. Initiative measures a child's ability to act in a manner that gets his/her needs met. Attachment measures a child's adaptive abilities to form healthy bonds with adults, and Self-Control measures a child's ability to regulate his/her behavior. To be developmentally sensitive, there are separate forms for infants, toddlers, and preschoolers. Psychometric analyses indicated that the DECA subscales have solid internal consistency and reliability (Brinkman, Wigent, Tomac, Pham, & Carlson, 2007).

Background information. Demographic questionnaires were completed for MHCs, educators, and children to gather information including age, race/ethnicity, and gender. In addition, MHCs completed the Consultant Background Questionnaire, which asked about their professional backgrounds, perceived areas of content expertise, and perceptions of their role. These two background measures were used to gather information for the three moderators used in the current analysis: child race/ethnicity, MHC expertise in cultural diversity, and MHC-educator ethnic match. The dichotomous variable for "boy of color" indicated whether a child was both male and belonging to an ethnic minority group (i.e., any race/ethnicity other than White). MHC expertise in cultural diversity was a self-reported, dichotomous item. MHC-educator ethnic match indicated whether educators and MHCs both selected the same race/ethnicity category for themselves (e.g., both White, both Latino).

Data Analysis

SPSS version 22 was used to conduct all analyses. The research questions were addressed using t-tests, multilevel models (MLM), and moderation analyses within MLM. MLM was used because the data were nested and therefore violated the assumption of independence for linear models. The MLMs constructed in this study were random intercepts models. Continuous predictor and control variables were grand mean centered for ease of interpretation.

This modeling took place in a series of steps. First, to evaluate the link between the three race/culture variables and CA, three separate MLMs were created with CA as the dependent variable. Then, t-tests were used to explore change from baseline to 6 months in all outcome measures. Next, intraclass correlations (ICCs) were calculated for each dependent variable to determine if, in fact, outcomes variables were clustered by educator and/or MHC. Subsequently, the differences between baseline and 6-month values for each outcome measure were calculated to create change scores. Again, the three race/culture variables were entered as the independent variables of separate MLMs, and the scores at 6 months were entered as dependent variables.

Finally, potential moderation was explored, again within MLMs. CA was added as the predictor variable, and the baseline value of the dependent variable was added as a control variable. Building upon this framework, separate models were then created to test each combination of dependent variable and moderator by building models that included an interaction term. If the interaction term was significant, simple slopes analyses were used to determine the direction of the effect. Because the moderators were binary, a simple slopes analysis was conducted by running the model separately at both values of the moderator (zero and one).

Results

To address research question 1, multilevel models were created to assess whether the three race/culture variables predicted the strength of CA. Three separate models, one for each of the binary predictors, were created with CA as the dependent variable and MHC as the grouping variable. Results indicated that none of the three variables significantly predicted the strength of CA (p-values >.05). Of note, the educator-MHC racial/ethnic match variable was marginally significant ($b = .04$, $p = .073$), such that matched dyads had somewhat higher CA ratings.

To address research question 2, analyses were conducted to investigate whether the three binary race/culture variables predicted change in each outcome measure after 6 months of consultation. Initial explorations of the data with dependent t-tests indicated that all scores significantly changed from baseline to 6 months (see

Table 2). Next, each combination of binary race/culture and outcome variables was analyzed in a series of multilevel random intercepts models. Each model included one of the binary race/culture variables as an independent variable, 6-month scores on an ECMHC outcome as the dependent variable, and baseline scores on the same outcome as a control variable. Because intraclass correlations (ICCs) demonstrated that child-level variables were meaningfully clustered at the educator level (ICCs ranged from 0.15-0.32, all statistically significant), two-level MLMs were created to account for non-independence of children nested within educators. Results for all models were non-significant. Specifically, the effects of the three variables did not predict change in: educator-child closeness, educator-child conflict, classroom climate, educator self-efficacy, educator hopelessness, child attachment behaviors, child self-control, or child initiative.

To address research question 3, the three race/culture variables were analyzed as potential moderators of the impact of CA on outcomes. Separate MLMs were constructed for each combination of moderator and dependent variable, resulting in twelve total models. All models had two levels; some had child data on Level 1 and educator data on Level 2, while others had educator data on Level 1 and MHC data on Level 2. Each model controlled for baseline values of the dependent variable. Results are presented in Table 3 for educator/classroom outcomes after 6 months of the ECMHC intervention and in Table 4 for child-level outcomes after 6 months of the ECMHC intervention. Significant moderation effects are described below.

One moderator variable, which we referred to as "boy of color," was significant for two outcomes: educator-child closeness and educator self-efficacy. The direct link between CA and improvement in educator-child closeness was moderated by whether the focus child was a boy of color. Specifically, when the focus child was a boy of color, a stronger CA between MHC and educator predicted significantly greater gains in educator-child closeness, while this link was non-significant for focus children who were not boys of color.

Working with a focus child who was a boy of color also significantly moderated the direct link between CA and educator self-efficacy, such that there was a significant positive link between CA and growth in educator self-efficacy if the focus child was a boy of color.

Self-reported MHC cultural expertise moderated the association between CA and improvement in three outcomes: child attachment behaviors, negative indicators of classroom emotional climate (e.g., harsh discipline, over-stimulating physical environment), and educator self-efficacy. Among MHCs who rated themselves as experts in cultural diversity, there was a significant positive link between CA and improvement in the focus child's attachment behaviors. Additionally, MHC expertise in cultural diversity significantly moderated the relationship between CA and decline in negative indicators of classroom emotional climate, such that there was a stronger negative association between CA and negative climate when MHCs were experts in cultural diversity. Specifically, when MHCs were experts in cultural diversity, they appear more effective in using the alliance to produce larger reductions in negative classroom climate. Finally, MHC's cultural expertise was a marginally significant ($p = .056$) moderator of the link between CA and growth in educator self-efficacy. For MHCs who described themselves as having content expertise in cultural diversity issues, there was a significant positive direct link between CA and educator increases in self-efficacy. It is important to note that there were no statistically significant correlations between racial/ethnic background of MHC and whether they had self-reported expertise in topics related to culture and race.

MHC-educator racial/ethnic match was a significant moderator for only one model. When MHCs and educators were racially/ethnically matched, there was a significant positive link between CA and improvement in the focus child's attachment behaviors.

Discussion

The imperative and impetus to fund and establish ECMHC interventions across the country was based on racialized expulsion rate data (Gilliam, 2005; U.S. Department of Health and Human Services and U.S. Department of Education, 2014). However, until as recently as 2015, much of the work in ECMHC had not dealt explicitly with targeting disparities that exist in the emotional well-being, expulsion rates and disciplinary practices for young children of color—especially African-American and Latino children. As a field, we have yet to fully understand whether and how ECMHC closes the gap in discipline disparities for young children who are at risk of marginalization. This study attempted to explore these trends by investigating the interconnections between the CA, race and culture, and ECMHC outcomes.

The results of this study enhance our understanding of how ECMHC works and for whom. Prior theoretical and empirical work highlighted the role of the CA in eliciting positive changes for educators and children (Davis, 2018; Duran et al., 2009; Green et al., 2006). ECMHC may yield a greater impact when educators and MHCs have a warm, collaborative alliance where both parties contribute expertise. In related research, when main effects were calculated for all participants, CA predicted improvements in child attachment behaviors, educator-child closeness, classroom climate, and educator self-efficacy (Davis, 2018). The current study expands upon that idea by incorporating moderator variables related to race and culture.

The current study found that the main effects of the CA on child-and educator-level outcomes varied depending on some racial and cultural considerations. The CA was related to changes in specific outcomes for some subgroups of the full sample, while for others this alliance was not a meaningful predictor of change. The subgroups were defined by the racial and cultural context of ECMHC: 1) whether the focus child was a boy of color, 2) whether the MHC considered herself to have expertise in cultural diversity, and 3) whether the MHC and educator were racially/ethnically matched. Of note, these three variables were also explored as direct predictors of CA and of outcomes, but these associations were not supported by our analyses. Rather, these cultural variables meaningfully impacted the extent to which CA predicted outcomes.

Whether the focus child was a boy of color significantly moderated the link between the CA and improvements in educator-child closeness, and between the CA and improvements in educator self-efficacy. In other words, the CA significantly predicted those outcomes only when the focus of ECMHC was a boy of color. The alliance between the educator and MHC was positively associated with improvement in the bond between the educator and child, and the educator's confidence in her abilities, only when the focus child was a boy of color. These finding are striking in the light of the literature regarding educator relationships with boys of color that may be impacted by implicit biases, cultural mismatches between educators and children, low expectations based on deeply rooted racial socialization history in this country, and misguided preparation for a world filled with bias (Adamu & Hogan, 2015; Clark & Zygmunt, 2014; U.S. Department of Health and Human Services and U.S. Department of Education, 2014). Other research reported that early educators working with a MHC feel more supported and efficacious in the classroom (Brennan, Bradley, Allen, & Perry, 2008; Shivers, 2015), which may in turn increase educators' confidence that they can retain a child in that setting whom they may otherwise have recommended for suspension or expulsion. In addition, in consultation with MHCs, early educators may gain insight into that child's cultural background and/or contextual influences (Gilliam et al., 2016), perhaps expanding educator understanding and empathy and facilitating the increases in closeness.

The impact of the CA also depended on whether the MHC was an expert in cultural diversity. When MHCs considered themselves experts, a strong CA predicted greater improvement in child attachment behaviors as well as a steeper reductions in negative classroom practices. In other words, CA may be a driver of changes in attachment behaviors and negative classroom climate for the subgroup of dyads in which the MHC was also highly skilled in culturally responsive practices. Finally, when educators and MHCs were racially/ethnically matched, CA significantly predicted improved child attachment behaviors. To our knowledge, no research currently exists that has directly measured the influence of a MHC's previous expertise in race- and culture-related topics or even how their racial and ethnic background might influence the development of relationships with early educators.

Researchers are in the nascent stage of exploring and testing hypotheses for why ECMHC is particularly effective at reducing disparities in suspensions, expulsions and other discipline practices (Gilliam et al., 2016; Shivers et al., manuscript in preparation). Experts in ECMHC have theorized that central to the ECMHC theory of change (see Duran et al., 2009; Hunter et al., 2016) is the focus on changes in adults' knowledge, attitudes, and behaviors, in contrast with a focus on pathology within an individual child or family. This stance then leads to improved communication among child care staff and parents. It also facilitates educator and administrator exploration regarding the meaning of individual children's behaviors as well as the developmental appropriateness of their expectations. National leaders in ECMHC have hypothesized that this combination of approaches works to minimize micro-aggressions and bias toward all children and especially children of color.

Limitations

As with all research endeavors, the current study has strengths and weaknesses. In terms of measurement, some variables were assessed using tools of unknown psychometric properties. The decisions to use these measures reflected clinical utility as well as the evolution of the research questions after data collection was complete. Specifically, a single-item indicator was used for measuring the complex constructs of CA and MHC cultural expertise. The Preschool Mental Health Climate Scale, while used widely in the ECMHC evaluation literature, has not been subject to rigorous psychometric testing. Hence, these results should be interpreted as exploratory and should be replicated using other validated measures.

Next, all of the multilevel models had significant levels of unexplained variance in the dependent variables, above and beyond the variance accounted for by the parameters. Because educator and child functioning have many influences, only some of which were measured here, it is unsurprising that these models did not account for all of the variance in these constructs. For instance, a child's attachment behaviors cannot be fully understood without including multiple parameters, including their attachment to their parents and other caregivers. It is also important to note that, by creating a series of separate models to test specific relationships, there was an increased risk for Type 1 error. In addition, there was not sufficient power to run MLMs with random slopes, which would have provided additional information regarding variation among educators or MHCs in the strength of the relationships detected between independent variables, dependent variables, and moderators.

Further, these results most likely reflect, to some extent, the impact of the specific context. For instance, the structure of child care, the demographics, and local policies/regulations may all be unique to this southwestern state. So, these results cannot be expected to generalize across all locations. Finally, these results reflect data gathered from educator-child dyads that were intact after 6 months of consultation—a subset of the initial sample of dyads in the study at baseline. Although there were missing data from dyads that were no longer in the sample, there were no significant differences between the initial sample and the 6-month sample on baseline characteristics.

Future Directions

The findings in this study as well as other emerging ECMHC research agendas indicate that applying a racial equity lens in ECMHC research and evaluations will allow us to gain deeper understanding of the mechanisms, predictors, and pathways to more equitable results in our ECMHC programs. Racial equity-informed research and evaluations are also necessary to ensure accountability at the systems level. Future research directions include improving measurement of CA to capture its nuances and to address different aspects of alliance, including mutual goals, trust, and collaboration. In addition, a racial equity informed research agenda for ECMHC should seek to answer questions such as how to attract and retain a diverse and culturally competent workforce of MHCs, and how to promote MHC relationship-building capabilities. Finally, it is critical to specify empirically whether the observed changes for boys of color translate into reductions in expulsion, as suggested by prior research. Additionally, research and data should be designed to help ensure accountability that the impact of ECMHC systems and programs is equitable for children and families of diverse racial, ethnic, cultural, and linguistic backgrounds and for families of diverse socio-economic statuses. Overall, it is necessary to continue to build upon this study to determine how best to prevent early childhood expulsion to enhance the ideal of early education as a driver of equity.

Table 1.
Participant Characteristics, n(%) or Mean (standard deviation)

		Educator (n = 289)	MHC (n = 62)
Age (years)		M = 37.29 (SD = 12.36)	M = 40.37 (SD = 10.58)
Years experience		M = 11.00 (SD=8.38)	M = 6.08 (SD = 6.89)
Gender			
	Female	284 (98.3%)	58 (93.5%)
	Male	5 (1.7%)	4 (6.5%)
Race/ethnicity			
	White	172 (59.7%)	46 (74.2%)
	Hispanic/Latino	79 (27.4%)	9 (14.5%)
	African American/Black	18 (6.3%)	4 (6.5%)
	Asian	6 (2.1%)	2 (3.2%)
	Native American	6 (2.1%)	0
	Other	7 (2.4%)	1 (1.6%)
Education			
	Some high school	2 (0.7%)	0
	High School graduate/GED	156 (54.2%)	0
	CDA	27 (9.4%)	0
	AA	37 (12.8%)	0
	BA/BS	52 (18.1%)	0
	MA/MS	11 (3.8%)	59 (95.2%)
	Doctoral degree	0	3 (4.8%)
	Other	3 (1.0%)	0

Table 2.
Dependent T-Test of Primary Outcome Measures from Baseline to Six Months

Measure	Means		T-value
	Baseline	*Six months*	
PMHCS positive indicators	3.36	3.76	-12.71**
PMHCS negative indicators	1.76	1.58	7.43**
Educator self-efficacy	4.07	4.19	-5.21**
Educator hopeless/overwhelmed	2.06	1.82	8.84**
Child attachment	2.63	2.94	-9.09**
Child self-control	1.78	2.23	-10.54**
Child initiative	2.11	2.47	-9.07**
Educator-child closeness	3.84	4.25	-11.68**
Educator-child conflict	2.95	2.61	7.17**

Table 3.
Multilevel Moderation Models for Educator/Classroom Outcomes

	Educator Self-efficacy	Hopeless/overwhelmed	Negative classroom climate	Positive classroom climate
Intercept	4.19**	1.80**	1.63**	3.67**
IV: Consultative Alliance	.17	-.16	-.53**	.99**
Control: Baseline DV	.37**	.58**	.36**	.54**
Moderator: Boy of color	-.05	.02	.02	-.06
Interaction: CA*BOC	.37*	-.07	-.08	.253
Intercept	4.17**	1.82**	1.64**	3.63**
IV: Consultative Alliance	.06	-.25	-.29*	.85**
Control: Baseline DV	.37**	.60**	.36**	.53**
Moderator: MHC cultural expertise	-.00	-.02	-.00	.00
Interaction: CA* MHC cultural expertise	.35	.08	-.40*	.23
Intercept	4.20**	1.86**	1.62**	3.63**
IV: Consultative Alliance	.25*	-.32	-.43**	1.0**
Control: Baseline DV	.37**	.60**	.37**	.54**
Moderator: Ethnic Match	-.06	-.08	.03	.01
Interation: CA*EM	.12	.23	-.21	.10

Table 4.
Multilevel Moderation Models for Child Outcomes

	Educator Self-efficacy	Hopeless/ over- whelmed	Negative classroom climate	Positive classroom climate
Intercept	4.26**	2.99**	2.53**	2.26**
IV: Consultative Alliance	.23	.27	.01	.25
Control: Baseline DV	.48**	.53**	.59**	.55**
Moderator: Boy of color	.03	-.07	-.12	-.09
Interaction: CA*BOC	.52*	.23	.42	.20
Intercept	4.29**	2.95**	2.55**	2.27**
IV: Consultative Alliance	.30	-.12	.05	.23
Control: Baseline DV	.47**	.53**	.62**	.59**
Moderator: MHC cultural expertise	-.03	.01	-.08	-.07
Interaction: CA* MHC cultural expertise	.07	.62*	.27	.11
Intercept	4.27**	2.90**	2.47**	2.21**
IV: Consultative Alliance	.26	.03	.23	.13
Control: Baseline DV	.47**	.55**	.60**	.56**
Moderator: Ethnic Match	-.03	.10	.03	.01
Interation: CA*EM	.20	.54*	.11	.31

References

Adamu, M., & Hogan, L. (2015). Point of entry: The preschool to prison pipeline. *Center for American Progress*. Retrieved from https://www.americanprogress.org/issues/criminal-justice/report/2015/10/08/122867/point-of-entry/

American Academy of Pediatrics. (2013). Out-of-school suspension and expulsion. *Pediatrics, 131*(3), e1000–e1007. Retrieved from https://doi.org/10.1542/peds.2012-3932

American Psychological Association Zero Tolerance Task Force. (2008). Are zero tolerance policies effective in the schools? An evidentiary review and recommendations. *The American Psychologist, 63*(9), 852–862. Retrieved from https://doi.org/10.1037/0003-066X.63.9.852

Barbarin, O. A. (2007). Mental health screening of preschool children: Validity and reliability of ABLE. *American Journal of Orthopsychiatry, 77*, 402–418. doi:10.1037/0002-9432.77.3.402

Barbarin, O. A., Murry, V. M., Tolan, P., & Graham, S. (2016). Development of boys and young men of color: Implications of developmental science for My Brother's Keeper Initiative. *SRCD Social Policy Report, 29*(3). Retrieved from http://www.srcd.org/sites/default/files/documents/spr_29_3_final.pdf

Barnett, S., Carolan, M., & Johns, D. (2013). *Equity and excellence: African-American children's access to quality preschool*. New Brunswick, NJ: National Institute for Early Education Research. Retrieved from http://nieer.org/sites/nieer/files/Equity%20and%20Excel

Brennan, E. M., Bradley, J. R., Allen, M. D., & Perry, D. F. (2008). The evidence base for mental health consultation in early childhood settings: Research synthesis addressing staff and program outcomes. *Early Education & Development, 19*(6), 982–1022. Retrieved from https://doi.org/10.1080/10409280801975834

Brinkman, T. M., Wigent, C. A., Tomac, R. A., Pham, A. V., & Carlson, J. S. (2007). Using the Devereux Early Childhood Assessment to identify behavioral risk and protective factors within a Head Start population. *Canadian Journal of School Psychology, 22*(2), 136–151. Retrieved from https://doi.org/10.1177/0829573507307612

Clark, P., & Zygmunt, E. (2014). A close encounter with personal bias: Pedagogical implications for teacher education. *The Journal of Negro Education, 83*(2), 147–161.

Cohen, E., & Kaufmann, R. K. (2000). *Early childhood mental health consultation*. DHHS Pub. No. CMHS-SVP0151. Rockville, MD: Center for Mental Health Services, Substance Abuse and Mental Health Services Administration.

Cohen, E., & Kaufmann, R. K. (2005). *Early childhood mental health consultation* (Rev. ed.). DHHS Pub. No. CMHS-SVP0151. Rockville, MD: Center for Mental Health Services, Substance Abuse and Mental Health Services Administration.

Davis, A. E. (2018). *The role of Consultative Alliance in Early Childhood Mental Health Consultation.* (Doctoral dissertation). Retrived from Proquest Dissertations & Theses.

Duran, F., Hepburn, K., Irvine, M., Kaufmann, R., Anthony, B., Horen, N., & Perry, D. (2009). *What works? A study of effective early childhood mental health consultation programs.* Washington, DC: Georgetown University Center for Child and Human Development.

Geller, S., & Lynch, K. (1999). *Teacher Opinion Survey.* Richmond, VA: Virginia Commonwealth University Intellectual Property Foundation and Wingspan, LLC.

Gilliam, W. S. (2005). *Prekindergarteners left behind: Expulsion rates in state prekindergarten systems.* New Haven, CT: Yale University Child Study Center.

Gilliam, W. S. (2008). *Preschool Mental Health Climate Scale.* Unpublished instrument, Yale University, Child Study Center, New Haven, CT.

Gilliam, W. S., Maupin, A. N., & Reyes, C. R. (2016). Early childhood mental health consultation: Results of a statewide random-controlled evaluation. *Journal of the American Academy of Child & Adolescent Psychiatry, 55*(9), 754–761. Retrieved from https://doi.org/10.1016/j.jaac.2016.06.006

Gilliam, W. S., Maupin, A. N., Reyes, C. R., Accavitti, M., & Shic, F. (2016) *Do early educators' implicit biases regarding sex and race relate to behavior expectations and recommendations of preschool expulsions and suspensions?* New Haven, CT: Yale University Child Study Center. Retrieved from http://ziglercenter.yale.edu/publications/Preschool%20Implicit%20Bias%20Policy%20Brief_final_9_26_276766_5379.pdf

Green, B. L., Everhart, M., Gordon, L., & Gettman, M. G. (2006). Characteristics of effective mental health consultation in early childhood settings: Multilevel analysis of a national survey. *Topics in Early Childhood Special Education, 26*(3), 142–152. Retrieved from http://doi.org/10.1177/02711214060260030201_

Harvard University Center on the Developing Child (2018). *Frontiers of Innovation.* Retrieved from https://developingchild.harvard.edu/innovation-application/frontiers-of-innovation/

Hepburn, K. S., Perry, D. F., Shivers, E. M. & Gilliam, W. S. (2013). *early childhood mental health consultation as an evidence-based practice: Where does it stand?* Washington DC: ZERO TO THREE.

Hunter, A., Davis, A.E., Perry, D.F., & Jones, W. (2016). *Manual: Early Childhood Mental Health Consultation in Early Childhood Educational Settings.* Washington, DC: Georgetown University Center for Child and Human Development.

Johnston, K., & Brinamen, C. F. (2012). The consultation relationship—From transactional to transformative: Hypothesizing about the nature of change. *Infant Mental Health Journal, 33*(3), 226–233. Retrieved from https://doi.org/10.1002/imhj.21332

Johnston, K., & Brinamen, C. (2006). *Mental health consultation in child care: Transforming relationships among directors, staff, and families.* Washington, DC: ZERO TO THREE.

Kirwan Institute. (2015). *State of the science: Implicit bias review 2015.* With funding from the W.K. Kellogg Foundation. Retrieved from: http://kirwaninstitute.osu.edu/wp-content/uploads/2015/05/2015-kirwan-implicit-bias.pdf

LeBuffe, P. A., & Naglieri, J. A. (1999). *Devereux early childhood assessment: Technical manual.* Lewisville, NC: Kaplan Early Learning Company.

LeBuffe, P.A., & Naglieri, J. A. (2003). *Devereux Early Childhood Assessment Clinical Form* (DECA-C). Lewisville, NC: Kaplan Early Learning Company.

Mackrain, M., & LeBuffe, P.A. (2007). *Devereux Early Childhood Assessment—Infant/Toddler Form* (DECA-I/T). Lewisville, NC: Kaplan Early Learning Company.

Magnuson, K., & Shager, H. (2010). Early education: Progress and promise for children from low-income families. *Children and Youth Services Review, 32*(9), 1186–1198. Retrieved from https://doi.org/10.1016/j.childyouth.2010.03.006

McCann, C., Shivers, E. M., & Means, K. (2018). *Preventing expulsion and suspension, promoting equity and the relationship to quality improvement.* Paper presentation, QRIS National Meeting, San Diego, CA.

McDonald, J.H. (2014). *Handbook of biological statistics* (3rd ed.). Baltimore, MD: Sparky House Publishing.

Meek, S.E., & W.S. Gilliam. (2016). *Expulsion and suspension as matters of social justice and health equity.* Discussion Paper, National Academy of Medicine, Washington, DC. Retrieved from https://nam.edu/wp-content/uploads/2016/10/Expulsion-and-Suspension-in-EarlyEducation-as-Matters-of-Social-Justice-and-HealthEquity.pdf.

My Brother's Keeper Task Force. (2016). *My Brother's Keeper 2016 progress report*: Two years of expanding opportunity and creating pathways to success. Retrieved from https://www.whitehouse.gov/sites/whitehouse.gov/files/images/MBK-2016-Progress-Report.pdf

Okonofua, J. A., & Eberhardt, J. L. (2015). Two strikes: Race and the disciplining of young students. *Psychological Science, 26*(5), 617–624. Retrieved from https://doi.org/10.1177/0956797615570365

Pianta, R. (2001). *Student–teacher relationship scale–short form*. Lutz, FL: Psychological Assessment Resources.

Raible, J., & Irizarry, J. G. (2010). Redirecting the teacher's gaze: Teacher education, youth surveillance and the school-to-prison pipeline. *Teaching and Teacher Education 26*, 1196–1203.

Reardon, S. F., & Portilla, X. A. (2016). Recent trends in income, racial, and ethnic school readiness gaps at kindergarten entry. *AERA Open*. doi:10.1177/2332858416657343.

Sheridan, S. M., Rispoli, K. M., & Holmes, S. R. (2014). Treatment integrity in conjoint behavioral consultation: Active ingredients and potential pathways of influence. In L. Sanetti, T. Kratochwill (Eds.), *Treatment integrity: A foundation for evidence-based practice in applied psychology* (pp. 255–278). Washington, DC: American Psychological Association.

Shivers, E. M. (2015). *Arizona's Smart Support evaluation report: The first four years*. Phoenix, AZ: Indigo Cultural Center and Southwest Human Development, with support from First Things First.

Shivers, E. M., Farago, F., Guimond, A., & Steier, A. (manuscript in preparation). What about the gap? Effects of children's gender and race in child care mental health consultation.

Substance Abuse and Mental Health Services Administration. (2014). *Expert convening on infant and early childhood mental health consultation*. Rockville, MD: SAMHSA Headquarters.

Tenenbaum, H. R., & Ruck, M. D. (2007). Are teachers' expectations different for racial minority than for European American students? A meta-analysis. *Journal of Educational Psychology, 99*(2), 253.

U.S. Department of Education, Office of Civil Rights. (2016). *2013-2014 Civil rights data collection: Key data highlights on equity and opportunity gaps in our nation's public schools*. Retrieved from http://www2.ed.gov/about/offices/list/ocr/docs/2013-14-first-look.pdf

U.S. Department of Health and Human Services and U.S. Department of Education. (2014). *Policy statement on expulsion and suspension policies in early childhood settings*. Retrieved from http://www2.ed.gov/policy/gen/guid/school-discipline/policy-statement-ece-expulsions-suspensions.pdf.

Knowledge and Perceptions Related to Evidence-Based Behavioral Interventions Among Early Childhood Educators

Adrienne Garro, Rachel Pess, and Nicolette Rittenhouse-Young

Abstract

The percentage of young children with significant behavioral challenges is concerning, with some prevalence rates as high as 15% (Fox & Smith, 2007). While there are a number of evidence-based interventions to address behavioral problems in young children, several obstacles interfere with implementation. One prominent obstacle is lack of knowledge of evidence-based practice (EBP) among early childhood educators, who are often the most likely to manage directly behavioral challenges but who also feel ill-equipped to manage them. There has been relatively little research looking at educators' familiarity with EBP, particularly among staff who work in early childhood settings. The present study sought to address this gap by examining knowledge and perceptions related to EBP in a sample of teachers and assistant teachers from community-based daycares and preschools. Results indicated that, overall, a significant percentage of these educators were not familiar with EBP in general, and a high number lacked familiarity with specific EBP behavioral interventions. This study also examined background variables that might be related to educator knowledge of EBP. Continued research in these areas is vital to better support early childhood educators' use of EBP interventions.

Keywords: **evidence-based practice (EBP), behavioral interventions, early childhood educators**

It is well documented that many children in early learning programs display challenging behaviors. Research suggests that 9–15% of young children show significantly high levels of problem behavior, with higher rates among children who experience risk factors such as developmental delays and/or poverty (Fox & Smith, 2007; Kupersmidt, Bryant, & Willoughby, 2000; Qi & Kaiser, 2003). Within the past 15–20 years, a number of behavioral interventions, programs, and curricula have been developed to improve young children's behavior and social-emotional functioning. These vary with respect to their targets (e.g., children, parents, teachers/care providers or a combination of these), their settings (e.g., clinic, school), their mode of implementation (e.g., program-level, child-specific or combination), and other factors. Many of these interventions fit within the domain of evidence-based practice (EBP). The term "evidence-based" is typically used to describe a program or practice that has been examined thoroughly through research and found to be successful. While EBP is well-documented in school settings, it is also receiving increased emphasis in the field of early childhood. A brief review of several EB behavioral programs for younger children is provided below.

Promoting Alternative Thinking Strategies for Preschoolers (PATHS)

PATHS (Domitrovich, Cortes, & Greenberg, 2007) is a comprehensive curriculum designed to decrease behavioral and social-emotional problems and to increase social-emotional skills through teaching and activities focused on awareness and identification of emotions, sharing, problem-solving, friendship-building, and behavioral self-control (Domitrovich et al., 2007). Preschool PATHS has been examined through a number of studies and has demonstrated positive effects such as increased levels of teacher-reported social skills and higher levels of attentional skills, understanding of others' emotional perspectives, prosocial behavior, and emotion knowledge and vocabulary in comparison to control children (Arda & Ocak, 2012; Hamre, Pianta, Mashburn, & Downer, 2012; Hughes & Cline, 2015). In addition, some research has found that PATHS is effective in decreasing levels of behavior problems (e.g., Arda & Ocak, 2012), while other studies have not found this reduction but have yielded increases in positive behaviors (Hamre et al., 2012).

Preschool First Step to Success (PFS)

PFS is an intervention with classroom coaching to help teachers develop positive behavior management strategies as well as coaching for parents/families to teach skills related to communication, limit setting, gaining children's compliance, problem solving, etc. Several studies have yielded positive effects for PFS. For example, Feil et al. (2014) conducted a randomized controlled trial of PFS with 128 preschool children with externalizing problems and found that those who received the intervention showed higher social skills and lower levels of problem behavior in comparison to a control group. In follow-up research, Feil et al. (2016) examined PFS with a subgroup of their previous sample including children with ADHD symptoms. The results indicated positive effects on social skills and reductions in problematic behavior, including ADHD-related symptoms.

Positive Behavioral Interventions and Supports (PBIS)

PBIS refers to a tiered system of prevention and intervention that addresses children's behavioral problems with a focus on increasing prosocial and other appropriate behaviors. The first tier is primary prevention, which includes clearly defined behavioral expectations, explicit teaching, feedback to children about their behavior, and well-organized classrooms (Benedict, Horner, & Squires 2007; Stormont, Lewis, & Beckner, 2005). The second tier involves small-group interventions that target children with some risk factors (e.g., social skills problems) (Benedict et al., 2007; Hawken & Horner, 2003). The third tier addresses children with more intensive behavioral problems and consists of individualized interventions, which, ideally, should be generated from functional behavioral assessment (FBA).

A substantial body of research has examined PBIS in early childhood settings. When applied as a form of universal prevention, PBIS has been shown to increase child engagement and decrease levels of challenging behaviors (Blair, Fox, & Lentini, 2010; Snell et al., 2014). For young children who already demonstrate behavioral challenges, PBIS has shown reductions in aggressive and tantrum behavior (Blair et al., 2010; Dunlap & Fox, 1999; Umbreit & Blair, 1997). PBIS has been studied in a variety of settings, including Head Start Centers and community-based childcare programs, and results indicate a range of positive effects such as improved child engagement and reductions in disruptive conduct (Blair et al., 2010; Duda, Dunlap, Fox, Lentini, & Clarke, 2004; Snell et al., 2014). Despite the empirical support behind PBIS in early childhood settings, several challenges prevent more extensive implementation. These include variability in application, skepticism about practices, and need for more specific knowledge and skills of particular techniques (Fox, Jack, & Broyles, 2005; Frey, Park, Browne-Ferrigno, & Korfhage, 2010).

Incredible Years (IY)

Incredible Years (Webster-Stratton, 2000) is a set of interventions for children, parents and teachers that can be used on their own or in combination to improve social-emotional skills and prevent or decrease behavioral problems. The child version includes: a) the Classroom Dina Dinosaur curriculum, a prevention-based program delivered through modules and lesson plans by teachers or group leaders to children ages 3–8 years and b) the Small Group Dinosaur, a small-group treatment implemented by counselors/therapists for children who have psychological difficulties (Webster-Stratton, 2011). The teacher version consists of: a) the Teacher Classroom Management Program, implemented by group leaders who conduct teacher workshops to train in positive classroom management and b) Incredible Beginnings, also carried out in a group format for teachers and childcare providers and focusing on positive behavior management and social-emotional coaching. The parent version targets improvement in parent-child interactions, problem-solving skills, and communication and incorporates four programs based upon child age: baby, for birth to 12 months; toddler, for ages 1 to 3 years; preschooler, for ages 3 to 6 years; and school-age for ages 6 to 12 years. Over the past 10 years, IY has accumulated considerable empirical support through multiple studies including randomized controlled trials (e.g., Seabra-Santos et al., 2016; Perrin, Sheldrick, McMenamy, Henson, & Carter, 2014).

Obstacles and Challenges to EBP in Early Childhood Settings

Although research has generated a number of EB behavioral interventions for use in early childhood settings, there are continuing obstacles and challenges to their actual implementation. One of these is variability in standards and regulations across different settings (e.g., private daycare, Head Start centers, family childcare homes, etc.). For example, in some states, training and qualifications of staff in family childcare homes are not regulated and a specific curriculum is not required, while programs that are accredited by the National Association for the Education of Young Children (NAEYC) and Head Start/Early Start programs must meet specific quality standards across multiple areas (NAEYC, n.d.; U.S. Dept. of Health and Human Services, 2016). With respect to curriculum, both NAEYC and Head Start/Early Start call for developmentally appropriate content that encompasses particular domains including social relationships and emotional development. When it comes to teacher qualifications, NAEYC and Head Start/Early Start require their programs to have a minimum percentage of teachers with bachelor's degrees (75% and 50%, respectively). Outside of NAEYC-accredited and Head Start/Early Start programs, there is a lack of specific information regarding educational levels of staff who work with young children.

Other factors contribute to low utility of EB behavioral interventions in early childhood settings. Prominent among these is lack of training. A number of studies have found that early childhood educators express the need for more and/or improved training when it comes to addressing problem behaviors (Friedman-Krauss, Raver, Neuspiel, & Kinsel, 2014; Hemmeter, Corso, & Cheatham, 2006). In some settings, educators might be knowledgeable about general practices that facilitate appropriate behavior but have difficulty using individualized strategies for particular children (Muscott, Pomerleau, & Szczesiul, 2009). In a study of Head Starts from the mid-Atlantic region of the United States, Snell, Berlin, Voorhees, Stanton-Chapman, and Hadden (2012) found that, while teachers were generally knowledgeable about and reported using prevention-based strategies (e.g., establishment of rules and positive expectations), they were less likely to use individualized strategies for particular children and to try to determine the specific cause(s) of behavior problems. Similarly, Quesenberry, Hemmeter, and Ostrosky (2011) examined policies and procedures related to social-emotional development and challenging behaviors in a small study of Head Start centers. Results indicated that, when it came to "supporting children with persistent challenging behavior," only one of six centers was rated highly, while the others scored low. The above research suggests that even in Head Start programs, which require higher educator credentials than private programs, there is a need for additional support to facilitate the use of effective behavioral interventions.

Educator Knowledge, Perceptions, and Experiences with EBP

Research examining knowledge and perceptions of teachers related to EBP is scarce. In a study of general education teachers from elementary and preschool levels, Stormont, Reinke, and Herman (2011) found that 82–92% had not heard of nine out of ten of the EB interventions that were presented, such as the Good Behavior Game, PATHS, Triple P, and Incredible Years. Among these interventions, only PBIS was recognized by the majority of the sample. Research conducted by Pribble (2013) examined training experiences, level of preparedness, and implementation practices of preservice early childhood teachers. Overall, the results indicated that these teachers felt slightly to moderately prepared when it came to implementing social-emotional and behavioral assessment. Almost 67% had been required to take a course in behavior management, and 89% were required to take an assessment course, though only 28.5% were taught to administer some type of social-emotional assessment. Pribble also found variable implementation of different behavior strategies, with the most common being: use of positive feedback and encouragement; labeling of emotions; modeling of positive behaviors and development of consistent, balanced schedules and routines to prevent difficult behaviors. Based upon these results, Pribble concluded that early childhood teachers need more comprehensive training in behavioral assessment and intervention.

The Present Study

Given the research gaps described above and the continuing challenges to use of EB behavioral interventions in early childhood programs, the present study sought to examine knowledge and perceptions related to such interventions and to EBP in general. Another primary aim was to gather data from a sample of educators who work in community-based daycares and preschools since there is little research focusing on this population. The current study addressed the following research questions: a) Are early-childhood teachers familiar with "evidence-based practice/intervention?" b) Are early-childhood teachers aware of behavioral interventions in their schools/centers and do these interventions fit the definition of EB practice? c) What are early-childhood teachers' levels of familiarity with specific EB behavioral interventions? and d) What background variables are associated with early-childhood teachers' knowledge/familiarity with EB practice/interventions?

Methods
Procedures

Procedures and the measure used for this study were approved by the university Institutional Review Board where the researchers were located. Participants for this study were recruited through two main mechanisms: the website of NAEYC and flyers distributed via email among several childcare centers in the states of NJ and PA. In the case of NAEYC, the researchers obtained permission to contact members via email to provide information about the study. The original set of data collected through NAEYC examined knowledge and perceptions of early childhood personnel who worked in a variety of roles (e.g., teachers, directors, etc.) from a wider range of settings (e.g., private daycares, Head Start centers, etc.). For the purposes of the current project, a subset of this data including only teachers and teaching assistants who worked in private daycares or preschools was examined. Furthermore, the recruitment that took place through flyer distribution was targeted toward teachers and assistants in these settings only. The decision to reduce the dataset according to these parameters was based on the desire to gather data from educators who were most likely to directly deal with young children's behavioral difficulties. In addition, Head Start centers and public preschool programs are more likely to have funding devoted to behavioral and mental-health needs. As a result, educators who work in these settings are assumed to have greater exposure to EB strategies, which could potentially skew the research sample.

Early-childhood educators who were interested in participating in the study were sent an electronic link to the research survey, which was administered via Qualtrics, an online program which allows for non-trackable responses. Thus, participants were able to complete the survey privately and at their convenience.

Measure

A single online survey was created by the researchers for this study. The first section included background and demographic items (e.g., gender, age, education level, job position, etc.). The second section of the survey included a variety of items that examined participants' knowledge and opinions regarding EBP, behavioral interventions, and early childhood curricula including use in their own center/school. The third section provided a list of 18 EB early-childhood interventions that focus on behavior or social-emotional development and asked participants to indicate their degree of familiarity for each one ("not familiar," "somewhat familiar," or "very familiar"). Ten interventions came from Powell and Dunlap's 2009 publication, *Evidence-Based Social-Emotional Curricula and Intervention Packages for Children 0-5 Years and Their Families*. The other eight programs were chosen based upon review of research using search terms such as "evidence-based early childhood curricula" and "evidence-based interventions for young children." Interventions were included if they had at least two research studies providing support in the form of significant positive change from pre-test to post-test or significantly better outcomes when evaluated against a comparison group.

Sample

A total of 44 participants completed the survey questions. An examination of the demographic data indicated that all of the educators were female. In terms of race, 36 participants (81.8% of the sample) identified as Caucasian/White; three identified as Latina (6.8%); three identified as Asian American (6.8%); and two identified as African American (4.5%). None of the sample identified as "other" or "mixed race." The median age of participants was 37 years. Participants indicated their highest level of completed education and types of certification they had attained (if any). Twenty participants had bachelors' degrees (45.5% of sample), eight participants had masters' degrees (18.2%), eleven participants attended some college or acquired an associate's degree (25%), four participants had attained a high school diploma or GED (9.1%), and one participant was still in high school (2.3%). Sixteen participants had either early childhood or elementary education certification in their state (36.4%

of sample), six participants had their Child Development Associate (CDA) credential (13.6%), and the remaining 50% indicated no educational certification. Most of the participants (32 or 72.7% of the sample) were teachers in community-based daycares or preschools and the remaining 12 participants were assistant teachers (27.3%).

Data Analysis

This study was exploratory and involved both descriptive analyses and non-parametrical statistical tests. When examining familiarity with "evidence-based practice/intervention" and whether behavioral interventions were used in their centers/schools, the percentages of educators endorsing "yes" or "no" were calculated. For the question, "Does your school or center use behavioral interventions or strategies that have been proven by research to be equal to or better than other strategies or services?" percentages responding "yes," "no," or "not sure" were calculated. The "not sure" choice was added to take into account educators' possible lack of detailed knowledge about their schools'/centers' behavioral interventions. Percentages also described levels of familiarity with each of the 18 EB behavioral interventions that were listed.

Given the emphasis placed on education and qualifications of early childhood personnel in both policy and practice, the researchers examined educational level and presence/absence of educational certification as two variables that might be associated with knowledge of the term "evidence-based practice/intervention." To examine these relationships, two chi-square tests were used. The relationships between these same two variables and levels of familiarity with the 18 specific EB interventions were examined using Mann-Whitney U tests. For these analyses, the variable of educational level, which was originally divided into five categories, was collapsed into two categories—those having a bachelor's or master's degree and those having less than a bachelor's degree. The variable related to certification was also coded dichotomously as either having some type of state educational certification or not. Participants who had a CDA only were coded as not having a certification. Supplemental analyses were conducted to look at potential relationships between other sets of variables.

Results

Table 1 shows the percentages of participants responding "yes," "no," and, when applicable, "unsure" to questions about familiarity with EBP, their centers' use of behavioral interventions, and the type of behavioral interventions applied in their centers. The results illustrated that a little more than one-third of participants were not familiar with the term "evidence-based" practice/intervention and slightly less than two-thirds were familiar with it. Almost 73% of participants indicated that their school/center used behavioral interventions or strategies. However, when asked if their school or center used behavioral interventions that were "proven by research to be equal or better than other strategies," which is a commonly applied definition for EBP, only 25% of participants answered affirmatively. Almost 66% of the sample endorsed that they were unsure in response to this question. The above results suggest that, while a significant percentage of our sample had general familiarity with EB practice and were aware if their school/center used behavioral interventions, a relatively high number of them were not certain if their school/center's behavioral interventions were EB.

Table 2 shows participants' familiarity with specific EB behavioral interventions. For each one, participants responded on an ordinal scale: "very familiar," "somewhat familiar," or "not familiar." These results indicated that PBIS was most familiar to participants, with 50% indicating some degree of familiarity. This was followed by Schools and Families Educating (SAFE) Children, with 34.1% indicating some degree of familiarity; PATHS, with 31.8% indicating some degree of familiarity; Preschool "I Can Problem Solve," with 27.3% indicating some degree of familiarity; and Open Circle and Social Skills in Pictures, Stories and Songs, both with 25% of participants endorsing some degree of familiarity. The results from Table 2 also indicated that there are a number of EB behavioral interventions which, in general, were not familiar to educators. For example, over 90% of participants indicated that the Triple P program, Incredible Years/Dina Dinosaur, Al's Pals, Project ACHIEVE, and Coping Cat were not familiar to them. Over 80% of participants were not familiar with First Step to Success, Second Step, Coping Power, Pre-K FAST, the Olweus Anti-Bully Program, and the Emotions Course. In total, the above results suggest that familiarity with EB behavioral interventions in this sample was relatively low.

The next set of analyses focused on the relationships between the variables of educational level and presence/absence of certification and educators' knowledge/familiarity as described above. The result from the first chi-square investigating the relationship between educational level and familiarity with "evidence-based practice/intervention" was significant $X_2 (1, N = 44) = 5.49\ p = .049$. Thus, familiarity varied to a statistically significant degree between educators with less than a bachelor's degree and those with a bachelor's or master's degree. Higher educational level was associated with greater familiarity with EBP. The result from the second chi-square looking at the relationship between presence/absence of certification and familiarity with EBP was not significant $X_2 (1, N = 44) = .82\ p = .98$.

Table 1
Knowledge and Use Related to Evidence-Based Interventions and Behavioral Interventions

	Percentage of Participants		
	Yes	No	Unsure
Have you heard of the term "evidence-based practice" or "evidence-based intervention"?	31.8	68.2	N/A
Does your school or center use any types of behavioral interventions or strategies?	72.7	27.3	N/A
Does your school or center use behavioral interventions or strategies or services?	25	9.1	65.9

Table 2
Knowledge of Evidence-Based Behavioral Interventions and Programs

	Percentage of Participants		
	Not familiar	Somewhat familiar	Very familiar
Positive Behavior Supports (PBS)/Positive Behavior Interventions & Supports (PBIS)	50	40.9	9.1
Promoting Alternative Thinking Strategies (PATHS)	68.2	29.5	2.3
First Step to Success	81.8	13.6	4.5
Preschool "I Can Problem Solve"	72.7	20.5	6.8
Al's Pals	95.5	4.5	0
Second Step Program	81.8	9.1	9.1
Good Behavior Game	77.3	18.2	4.5
Incredible Years/Dina Dinosaur	95.5	4.5	0
Coping Power	88.6	11.4	0
Schools and Families Educating Children (SAFE Children)	65.9	27.3	6.8
Open Circle Curriculum	75.0	20.5	4.5
Coping Cat	97.7	0	2.3
Project ACHIEVE	90.9	6.8	2.3
Pre-K FAST	88.6	9.1	2.3
Triple P Program/Positive Parenting Program	93.2	6.8	0
Olweus Bullying Prevention Program	86.4	11.4	2.3
Social Skills in Pictures, Stories and Songs	75.0	20.5	4.5
Emotions Course	86.4	13.6	0

A total of 18 Mann-Whitney U tests were carried out to look at the relationships between educational level and familiarity with individual EB behavioral interventions, and then another 18 were conducted to examine the relationships between presence/absence of certification and familiarity with these same interventions. The results from the first set of tests found that educational level was not significantly associated with familiarity with any of the 18 interventions. Thus, participants with a bachelor's or master's degree did not show greater familiarity with any of the EB behavioral interventions. Similarly, the second set of Mann-Whitneys found that educational certification was not significantly associated with familiarity for any of the specific interventions. As supplementary analyses, another set of 18 Mann-Whitney U tests was carried out to look at the possible relationships between familiarity with the specific EB behavioral interventions and familiarity with the term "evidence-based practice/intervention" in general. The results found several significant positive associations. For example, educators who endorsed knowledge of the term "evidence-based practice/intervention" showed greater familiarity with PBS, PATHS, and SAFE Children. Thus, in this sample, general familiarity with EBP was linked to higher awareness of some specific EB behavioral interventions.

Table 3 shows participants' responses to other questions from section two of the survey which related to curriculum, training, and perceptions about school/center responsibilities. When it came to rating the effectiveness of their center/school curriculum in addressing children's behavioral needs, 56% agreed that it did so, and only two participants disagreed. However, it is notable that 31.3% of the sample expressed uncertainty about whether their curricula were effective in addressing children's behavioral needs. With respect to beliefs about whether centers/schools have a responsibility to address children's behavior problems in the classroom and to provide behavioral interventions to children, about 73% expressed some degree of agreement for each of these sentiments; 25% expressed uncertainty (neither agreed nor disagreed); and less than 5% disagreed.

Table 3
Knowledge and Perceptions Related to Early Childhood Curricula, Behavioral Problems and Behavioral Interventions

	Percentage of Participants				
	Strongly Agree	Agree	Neither Agree nor Disagree	Disagree	Strongly Disagree
I feel like my school's or center's curriculum is effective in addressing children's behavioral needs.	9.4	46.9	31.3	12.5	0
I feel adequately trained to implement behavioral interventions or strategies in the classroom or school.	6.8	31.8	36.4	25	0
I am interested in receiving training in the use of behavioral interventions of strategies in the classroom or school.	43.2	36.4	20.5	0	0
I feel it is the school's or center's responsibility to address behavioral problems in the classroom of school.	34.1	38.6	25.0	2.3	0
I feel it is the school's or center's responsibility to provide behavioral interventions to children.	31.8	38.6	20.5	4.5	0

Two other key items on this survey focused on training. In response to the item, "I feel adequately trained to implement behavioral interventions or strategies in the classroom or school," almost 39% of participants indicated agreement, and 25% indicated disagreement. The remaining 36% neither agreed nor disagreed. A second item looked at participants' interest in receiving training related to behavioral interventions. A high percentage of participants (79.6%) agreed or strongly agreed that they wanted this kind of training. No participants disagreed and 20.5% expressed uncertainty.

A chi-square analysis was used to examine the relationship between perceived adequacy of training, which was on an ordinal scale, and general familiarity with EBP, which was coded dichotomously. The result from this analysis was not significant $X2$ (2, $N = 44$) = 3.5 $p = .30$. A series of 18 Spearman rho correlations looked at the relationships between perceived adequacy of training and levels of familiarity with each of the EB behavioral interventions. Results indicated that higher perceived adequacy of training was linked to higher familiarity with the Good Behavior Game $r(44) = .31, p = .04$, SAFE Children $r(44) = .31, p = 039$, Coping Power program $r(44) = .32, p = .036$, and the Olweus Bullying Program $r(44) = .78, p = .043$. Thus, perceived adequate training related to behavioral interventions was associated with greater knowledge of some interventions in this sample.

Discussion

To our knowledge, this was the first study to examine familiarity with EBP in general and with specific EB behavioral interventions in a sample of educators from community-based child care settings. The results indicated that about one-third of these educators were not familiar with the term "evidence-based practice/intervention." While more than half of the sample was familiar with this term, it is concerning that a significant percentage was not familiar with it. The need for EBP in early-childhood settings has been highlighted in research, policy, and practice (e.g., Buysse & Wesley, 2006; U.S. Department of Health & Human Services, 2016). This need, perhaps, is even more pronounced in community childcare settings, which are not required to adhere to specific standards of quality for practice and personnel. Similarly, knowledge of specific EB behavior programs was limited according to our results. While 50% of participants had some familiarity with PBIS, the majority were unfamiliar with the rest of the interventions. These results are aligned with those of Stormont et al. (2011) who also found low teacher familiarity with EB interventions in one of the few previous studies to look at knowledge and perceptions of EB practice. Also, in support of Stormont et al.'s results, we found that PBIS was the intervention most known to teachers. Supplemental analyses found that early childhood educators who indicated familiarity with the term "evidence-based practice" were more likely to be acquainted with several of the EB behavioral interventions that were presented.

Approximately 70% of our sample agreed with the statements that centers/schools should address behavioral problems and/or provide behavioral interventions to children, 25% did not endorse opinions either way on these topics, and only a small percentage of participants disagreed. Because teacher beliefs can impact their use of behavior management practices and vice versa, more systematic investigation of such connections among early childhood educators is warranted. Another key finding is that, while nearly 73% of our sample indicated that their center/school used behavioral interventions, almost 66% reported that they were not sure if these interventions were EB. This result might be related to lack of knowledge of EBP in general and/or be reflective of the educators' lack of knowledge of specific practices in their centers. In addition, although 56% of participants endorsed that their center/school curriculum was effective in addressing children's behavioral needs, a sizable proportion (about 31%) were uncertain, and 12.5% disagreed. This uncertainty might reflect true difficulty in assessing the impact of curriculum on child behavior or not seeing such an impact. It might also reflect lack of sufficient knowledge of specific aspects of early childhood curricula that are intended to address social-emotional functioning. When it comes to training, less than half of our sample reported that they felt adequately trained to implement behavioral interventions (39%), 36% neither agreed nor disagreed, and 25% disagreed. A high percentage of participants reported being interested in receiving training in the use of behavioral interventions. These findings, in general, are congruent with those from previous studies showing that early-childhood caregivers express the need for more and better training to address the high level of challenging behaviors in their centers and schools (Friedman-Krauss et al., 2014; Hemmeter et al., 2006).

In examining background variables, we found that higher educational level was associated with higher familiarity with EB practice in general, though presence of an educational certification was not significant. Some previous research has found a link between educational level of caregivers and positive outcomes for young children and/or program quality (Bassok, 2013; Burchinal, Cryer, Clifford, & Howes, 2002; Zill et al., 2001). However, some studies have found no relationship between these variables, and recent research has proposed that the link between education and early-childhood outcomes is complex and potentially influenced by other factors (Bassok, 2013; Whitebook & Ryan, 2011; Zaslow, Tout, Halle, Whittaker, & Lavelle, 2010). The small sample and research design of the present study did not allow for examination of these possible mechanisms. In considering other variables that might be associated with knowledge of EB interventions, we also explored participants' perceived adequacy of training related to behavioral interventions. The results suggested that training was linked to familiarity with some EB behavioral interventions. Our data analysis did not focus on the specific types of training that teachers had been exposed to. It is possible that analysis of actual training in connection to familiarity with EB interventions might generate different results.

The results from the present study have several key implications for early-childhood practice. First, it is clear that educators continue to need more training related to EB interventions. While this conclusion seems straightforward, a more nuanced explanation is warranted. For example, it is crucial for early childhood teachers to learn not only about specific EB programs and the research that supports them but also to gain guided implementation experiences. Previous research has found that implementation support is a fundamental piece to help ensure successful application of EB interventions (Gable, Tonelson, Sheth, Wilson, & Park, 2012; Wood, Drogan, & Janney, 2013). Second, education and training related to EB behavioral interventions need to be ongoing processes that start at the pre-service level and continue throughout educators' careers. One or two courses related to behavior management and occasional professional development are often not sufficient for educators to address effectively the everyday behavioral challenges they encounter in their centers/schools.

Efforts to improve education and training must be multifaceted and occur at multiple levels. At the national level, changes to the CDA credential could have significant positive impacts. Currently, to obtain this credential, early childhood personnel must attain six competency standards, one of which is "To support social and emotional development and to provide positive guidance" (Council for Professional Recognition, 2017). EBP is not specifically cited as part of this domain, but demonstration of positive behavior management strategies could be included. State standards for pre-service training of early childhood educators must also be assessed and potentially modified to more fully cover EB behavioral interventions, especially in light of the high numbers of young children who are expelled from daycare or preschool due to behavioral difficulties.

Practitioners from psychology and special education can play an integral role in expanding EB training for early childhood educators. There are two main mechanisms through which this could occur. As a problem-solving process, early childhood mental health consultation (ECMHC) enables school psychologists, special educators, and other professionals to apply their skill sets and expertise related to behavioral assessment and intervention in collaborating with early childhood caregivers. ECMHC has been found to be effective in improving outcomes for young children, child care teachers/staff, and overall program quality (Perry, Allen, Brennan, & Bradley, 2010; Brennan, Bradley, Allen, & Perry, 2008). Second, coaching strategies represent a constructive avenue for early childhood educators to gain knowledge and experiences with EB behavioral interventions. While there is no single, widely accepted definition of coaching in early childhood, it is considered a form of experiential learning, often on-the-job, which is characterized by a structured set of actions and interactions such as collaborative planning, observations and modeling by a coach/guide, role-plays, reflection, and performance feedback (Artman-Meeker, Fettig, Barton, Penney, & Zeng, 2015). Thus, as a form of training, coaching provides multiple elements and opportunities for teachers to not only acquire knowledge regarding EB behavioral strategies but also to implement them in natural contexts. Coaching has been established as a useful tool for enhancing the skills of early-childhood educators and promoting positive outcomes for young children (Pianta et al., 2017; Twigg et al., 2013).

Limitations

One of the primary limitations of the current study is its small sample of 44 participants. Small sample size contributes to low power for statistical analyses and can reduce the chances of identifying true effects as well as decrease the likelihood that a statistically significant result reflects a true outcome. Thus, the results should be interpreted with caution. Another limitation is that this was a convenience sample comprised of educators who responded to our specific recruitment efforts. Our sample did have relatively high educational levels for educators working in private centers. Due to these factors, our results might not be generalizable to a wider population of early childhood educators. As previously noted, levels of familiarity with specific EB behavioral interventions were low, which means there was restricted range of values for these variables that might have impacted the validity of some analyses. The one measure used for this study poses additional limitations. More specifically, this was a single survey developed by the researchers, which has unknown psychometric characteristics. For this measure, we chose EB interventions based upon research review, but it is possible that the list we compiled did not include some EB strategies or programs for young children.

Future Directions

The results from the current study contribute increased understanding of knowledge and perceptions of EB behavioral practice among community-based early-childhood educators. Given the high number of children attending community-based daycares and preschools and the prevalence of significant behavioral difficulties, it is vital to obtain a clearer picture of what these educators do or do not know about EB interventions. We anticipate that these results, in combination with other research efforts, will help shape education and training for early-childhood educators, including interdisciplinary collaborative efforts. Given the limitations of the present study, future research should expand to include more educators, particularly those from community-based settings, which tend to be an underrepresented research population. Use of additional and/or alternative measures with known psychometric properties would be beneficial to build upon the data generated from this study and enhance validity of future research. In addition, it would be valuable to further examine factors that are potentially related to early-childhood educators' knowledge and perceptions of EB interventions and to unpack their mechanisms of influence. Overall, we believe the results from the present study in combination with future related research will pave the way for increased understanding of early-child educators' application of EB interventions/practice, which, in turn, may lead to actual expansion of these practices in early childhood settings.

References

Arda, T.B., & Ocak, S. (2012). Social competence and promoting alternative thinking strategies: PATHS preschool curriculum. *Educational Sciences: Theory and Practice*, 12(4) 2691–2698.

Artman-Meeker, K., Fettig, A., Barton, E.E., Penney, A., & Zeng, S. (2015). Applying an evidence-based framework to the early childhood coaching literature. *Topics in Early Childhood Special Education*, 35(3) 144–156. doi:10.1177/0271121415595550

Bassok, D. (2013). Raising teacher education levels in Head Start: Exploring programmatic changes between 1999 and 2011. *Early Childhood Research Quarterly, 28*(4), 831–842. doi:10.1016/j. ecresq.2013.07.004

Benedict, E.A., Horner, R.H., & Squires, J.K. (2007). Assessment and implementation of positive behavior support in preschools. *Topics in Early Childhood Special Education, 27*(3), 174–192.

Blair, K., Fox, L., & Lentini, R. (2010). Use of positive behavior support to address the challenging behavior of young children within a community early childhood program. *Topics in Early Childhood Special Education, 30*(2), 68–79. Retrieved from https://doi.org/10.1177/0271121410372676

Brennan, E.M., Bradley, J.R., Allen, M.D., & Perry, D.F. (2008) The evidence base for mental health consultation in early childhood settings: Research synthesis addressing staff and program outcomes. *Early Education and Development, 19*(6), 982–102.

Burchinal, M. R., Cryer, D., Clifford, R. M., & Howes, C. (2002). Caregiver training and classroom quality in child care centers. *Applied Developmental Science, 6*(1), 2–11.

Buysse, V., & Wesley, P.W. (2006). *Evidence-based practice in the early childhood field.* Washington, DC: ZERO TO THREE.

Council for Professional Recognition. (2017). *CDA Competency Standards.* Retrieved from http://www.cdacouncil.org/about/cda-credential/competency-standards

Domitrovich, C.E., Cortes, R.C., & Greenberg, M.T. (2007). Improving young children's social and emotional competence: A randomized trial of the preschool "PATHS" curriculum. *The Journal of Primary Prevention, 28*(2), 67–91. doi:10.1007/s10935-007-0081-0

Duda, M.A., Dunlap, G., Fox, L., Lentini, R., & Clarke, S. (2004). An experimental evaluation of positive behavior support in a community preschool program. *Topics in Early Childhood Special Education, 24*(3), 143–155. Retrieved fromhttps://doi.org/10.1177%2F02711214040240030201

Dunlap, G., & Fox, L. (1999). A demonstration of behavioral support for young children with autism. *Journal of Positive Behavior Interventions, 1*(2), 77–87. Retrieved from https://doi.org/10.1177%2F109830079900100202

Feil, E. G., Frey, A., Walker, H. M., Small, J. W., Seeley, J. R., Golly, A., & Forness, S. R. (2014). The efficacy of a home/school intervention for preschoolers with challenging behaviors: A randomized control trial of Preschool First Step to Success. *Journal of Early Intervention, 36,* 151–170. doi:10.1177/1053815114566090

Feil, E.G., Small, J. W., Seeley, J. R., Walker, H. M., Golly, A., Frey, A., & Forness, S. R. (2016). Early intervention for preschoolers at risk for attention-deficit/ hyperactivity disorder: Preschool First Step to Success. *Behavioral Disorders, 41*(2): 95-106. doi:10.17988/0198-7429-41.2.95

Fox, L., Jack, S., & Broyles, L. (2005). *Program-wide positive behavior support: Supporting young children's social-emotional development and addressing challenging behavior.* Tampa, FL: University of South Florida, Louis de la Parte Florida Mental Health Institute.

Fox, L., & Smith, B. J. (2007). Issue brief: Promoting social, emotional and behavioral outcomes of young children served under IDEA. *Challenging Behavior*. Retrieved from https://files.eric.ed.gov/fulltext/ED526382.pdf

Frey, A. J., Park, K. L., Browne-Ferrigno, T., & Korfhage, T. L. (2010). The social validity of program-wide positive behavior support. *Journal of Positive Behavior Interventions, 12,* 222-235. doi:10.1177/1098300709343723

Friedman-Krauss, A.H., Raver, C.C., Neuspiel, J.M., & Kinsel, J. (2014). Child behavior problems, teacher executive functions, and teacher stress in Head Start classrooms. *Early Education and Development, 25*(5), 681-702. doi:10.1080/10409289.2013.825190

Gable, R. A., Tonelson, S. W., Sheth, M., Wilson, C., & Park, K. L. (2012). Importance, usage, and preparedness to implement evidence-based practices for students with emotional disabilities: A comparison of knowledge and skills of special education and general education teachers. *Education and Treatment of Children, 35,* 499-519.

Hamre, B.K., Pianta, R.C., Mashburn, A.J., & Downer, J.T. (2012). Promoting young children's social competence through the preschool PATHS curriculum and My Teaching Partner professional development resources. *Early Education and Development, 23*(6), 809-832. Retrieved from https://www.learntechlib.org/p/88489/

Hawken, L.S., & Horner, R.H. (2003). Evaluation of a targeted intervention within a schoolwide system of behavior support. *Journal of Behavioral Education, 12*(3), 225-240. Retrieved from https://doi.org/10.1023/A:1025512411930

Hemmeter, M. L., Corso, R., & Cheatham, G. (2006). *Issues in addressing challenging behaviors in young children: A national survey of early childhood educators.* Paper presented at the Conference on Research Innovations in Early Intervention, San Diego, CA.

Hughes, C., & Cline, T. (2015). An evaluation of the preschool PATHS curriculum on the development of preschool children, *Educational Psychology in Practice, 31*(1), 73-85, doi:10.1080/02667363.2014.988327

Kupersmidt, J.B., Bryant, D., & Willoughby, M. T. (2000). Prevalence of aggressive behaviors among preschoolers in Head Start and community child care programs. *Behavioral Disorders, 26*(1), 42–52.

Muscott, H.S., Pomerleau, T., & Szczesiul, S. (2009). Large-scale implementation of program-wide positive behavioral interventions and supports in early childhood education programs in New Hampshire. *NHSA Dialog, 12*(2), 148–169

National Association for the Education of Young Children. (n.d.) *Early learning program accreditation.* Retrieved from https://www.naeyc.org/accreditation/early-learning-program-accreditation

Perrin, E.C., Sheldrick, C., McMenamy, J.M., Henson, B.S., & Carter, A.S. (2014). Improving parenting skills for families of young children in pediatric settings: A randomized clinical trial. *JAMA Pediatrics, 168*(1), 16–24. doi:10.1001/jamapediatrics.2013.2919

Perry, D.F., Allen, M.D., Brennan, E.M., & Bradley, J.R. (2010). The evidence base for mental health consultation in early childhood settings: A research synthesis addressing children's behavioral outcomes. *Early Education and Development, 21*(6), 795–824.

Pianta, R., Hamre, B., Downer, J., Burchinal, M., Williford, A., LoCasale-Crouch, J., Howes, C., ... Scott-Little, C. (2017). Early childhood professional development: Coaching and coursework effects on indicators of children's school readiness. *Early Education and Development, 28*(8), 956–975. Retrieved from https://doi.org/10.1080/10409289.2017.1319783

Powell, D., & Dunlap, G. (2009). *Evidence-based social-emotional curricula and intervention packages for children 0-5 years and their families (roadmap to effective intervention practices).* Tampa, FL: University of South Florida, Technical Assistance Center on Social Emotional Intervention for Young Children. Retrieved from http://www.shankerinstitute.org/sites/shanker/files/roadmap_2%20Fox.pdf

Pribble, L.M. (2013). *Early childhood preservice teachers' knowledge and application of social emotional assessment and intervention practices.* (Doctoral Dissertation). ProQuest. Retrieved from http://www.proquest.com/en-US/products/dissertations/individuals.shtml

Qi, H. C., & Kaiser, A. (2003). Behavior problems of preschool children from low-income families: Review of the literature. *Topics in Early Childhood Special Education, 23*(4), 188–216. Retrieved from http://dx.doi.org/10.1177/02711214030230040201

Quesenberry, A.C., Hemmeter, M.L., & Ostrosky, M.M. (2011). Addressing challenging behaviors in Head Start: A closer look at program policies and procedures. *Topics in Early Childhood Special Education, 30*(4), 209-220. Retrieved from https://doi.org/10.1177%2F0271121410371985

Seabra-Santos, M.J., Gaspar, M. F., Azevedo, A. F., Homem, T. C.,Guerra, J., Martins, V., Leitao, S., ... Moura-Ramos, M. (2016). Incredible Years parent training: What changes, for whom, how, for how long? *Journal of Applied Developmental Psychology, 44*, 93-104, Retrieved from https://doi.org/10.1016/j.appdev.2016.04.004

Snell, M.E., Berlin, R.A., Voorhees, M.D., Stanton-Chapman, T.L., & Hadden, S. (2012). A survey of preschool staff concerning problem behavior and its prevention in Head Start classrooms. *Journal of Positive Behavior Interventions, 14*(2), 98-107 Retrieved from https://doi.org/10.1177/1098300711416818

Snell, M.E., Voorhees, M. D., Walker, V. L., Berlin, R. A., Jamison, K. R., & Stanton-Chapman, T. L. (2014). A demonstration of the universal problem-solving approach to address children's inappropriate behavior in Head Start classrooms. *Topics in Early Childhood Special Education 34*(1) 4-15. doi:10.1177/0271121413491836

Stormont, M., Lewis, T.J., & Beckner, R. (2005). Positive behavior support systems: Applying key features in preschool settings. *Teaching Exceptional Children, 37*(6), 42-49.Retrieved from https://doi.org/10.1177/004005990503700605.

Stormont, M., Reinke, W., & Herman, K. (2011). Teachers' knowledge of evidence-based interventions and available school resources for children with emotional and behavioral problems. *Journal of Behavioral Education, 20*(2), 138-147. Retrieved from http://dx.doi.org/10.1007/s10864-011-9122-0.

Twigg, D., Pendergast, D., Fluckiger, B., Garvis, S., Johnson, G., & Robertson, J. (2013). Coaching for early childhood educators: An insight into the effectiveness of an initiative. *International Research in Early Childhood Education, 4*(1), 73-90.

Umbreit, J., & Blair, K.S. (1997). Using structural analysis to facilitate treatment of aggression and noncompliance in a young child at-risk for behavioral disorders. *Behavioral Disorders, 22*(2), 75-86.

U.S. Deptartment of Health and Human Services Head Start Administration for Children and Families Office of Head Start (2016). *Head Start program performance standards*. Retrieved from https://eclkc.ohs.acf.hhs.gov/sites/default/files/pdf/hspps-appendix.pdf

Webster-Stratton, C. (2000). The Incredible Years training series. *Office of Juvenile Justice and Delinquency Prevention Bulletin Review*. 1-24. Retrieved from https://www.ncjrs.gov/pdffiles1/ojjdp/173422.pdf

Webster-Stratton, C. (2011). *The Incredible Years parents, teachers and children's training series: Program content, methods, research and dissemination.* Seattle, WA: Incredible Years.

Whitebook, M., & Ryan, S. (2011). *Degrees in context: Asking the right questions about preparing skilled and effective teachers of young children* [Preschool Policy Brief, 22]. New Brunswick, NJ: National Institute for Early Education Research, Rutgers University. Retrieved from http://cscce.berkeley.edu/files/2011/DegreesinContext_2011.pdf

Wood, B. K., Drogan, R. R., & Janney, D. M. (2013). Early childhood practitioner involvement in functional behavioral assessment and function-based interventions. *Topics in Early Childhood Special Education, 34*(1), 16–26. Retrieved from https://doi.org/10.1177/0271121413489736

Zaslow, M., Tout, K., Halle, T., Whittaker, J. V., & Lavelle, B. (2010). *Toward the identification of features of effective professional development for early childhood educators.* Washington, DC: Child Trends. Retrieved from https://www2.ed.gov/rschstat/eval/professional-development/literature-review.pdf

Zill, N., Rsenick, G., Kwang, K., McKey, R. H., Clark, C., Pai-Samant, S., Connell, D. C., ... D'Elio, M. A. (2001). *Head Start FACES: Longitudinal findings on program performance. Third progress report.* Washington, DC: U.S. Department of Health and Human Services, Administration for Children and Families.

List of Contributors

Ann M. Berghout Austin, Ph.D., is Professor of Human Development and Family Studies at Utah State University. She received her Ph.D. in Child Development from Iowa State University in 1981 and has been a professor at USU ever since. Along with others, she successfully lobbied the state legislature to establish the Utah Office of Child Care, located in Workforce Services. In addition to her faculty role, she is the executive director for the Bridgerland CCRR, now known as the Bridgerland Care About Childcare. She brings to USU several million dollars each year for research and development projects in childcare quality and availability.

Stacy L. Bender, Ph.D., NCSP is a licensed psychologist and assistant professor at the University of Massachusetts Boston. She specializes in family intervention and family-school engagement for culturally diverse and underserved populations, mindfulness-based practices for parents and teachers, and risk and protective factors affecting social-emotional and behavioral development in early childhood.

John S. Carlson, Ph.D., is a Professor of School Psychology and Director of Clinical Training at Michigan State University. His clinical and research interests include selective mutism, preschool assessment, trauma, and school psychopharmacology. He is currently working with the Michigan Department of Health and Human Services to evaluate five evidence-based practice initiatives aimed at improving the mental health functioning of children and adolescents across the state.

Kim M. Cornell is the Owner and Creative Director of Curious Questioners, and the former Director of New Initiatives at Professional Impact NJ. She helps transform leaders into curious questioners who create possibilities. She has worked in the field of education for over 20 years. Kim has a BA in Fine Arts, MA in Counselor Education, and MA in Early Childhood and Family Studies Advanced Curriculum and Teaching. She can be reached at kim@curiousquestioners.com.

Anna E. Davis, M.A. is a Ph.D. candidate in Clinical Psychology at The Catholic University of America. Her research focuses on the evaluation and implementation of early childhood mental health supports for children from low-income backgrounds, including her dissertation which is titled "The Role of Consultative Alliance in Early Childhood Mental Health Consultation." Ms. Davis is currently a pre-doctoral intern at the University of Maryland School of Medicine where she provides evidence-based clinical services for children and families impacted by mental health difficulties and trauma.

Marina Donnelly, M.Ed., is an advanced doctoral school psychology student at the University of Massachusetts Amherst. She is passionate about the home-, school-, and community-based systems and practices that promote positive behavioral development in young children. Her current research and applied interests focus on implementation and evaluation of school-based parent education services, family-school collaboration, and the use of technology in supporting and partnering with families.

Adrienne Garro, Ph.D., is an Associate Professor in the Department of Advanced Studies in Psychology at Kean University and coordinator of the department's School Psychology Professional Diploma Program. She teaches and supervises students in both this program and the Psy.D. in Combined School-Clinical Psychology at Kean. Dr. Garro is also a licensed psychologist who conducts assessments with children and adolescents who experience a wide range of developmental disabilities and or chronic conditions. Dr. Garro's research and clinical interests include comprehensive and contextual assessment of young children, child and family responses to pediatric chronic health conditions and developmental disabilities, and mindfulness interventions for children, adolescents, and families. She has published in journals across a variety of disciplines including pediatric health care, early childhood, and school psychology.

Keri Giordano, Psy.D. is an Assistant Professor in the Department of Advanced Studies in Psychology at Kean University. She has been in the field of early childhood for 23 years, working in a variety of roles, including: director, assistant director, teacher, early interventionist, school psychologist, trainer, professor, and consultant. Dr. Giordano specializes in working with the birth to five population, their families, and the professionals who support them.

List of Contributors

Dr. Kayla Gordon is a postdoctoral fellow and acting clinical director at the May Institute in Randolph, Massachusetts. Her research and clinical interests include supporting students through a positive behavior support framework as well as the assessment and treatment of challenging behaviors among individuals with autism.

Dr. Angel Fettig is an assistant professor in Special Education at the University of Washington. Her research focuses on supporting the social-emotional development and reducing challenging behaviors for young children with or at risk for disabilities. Specifically, she examines factors that influence implementation and intervention fidelity for education professionals and caregivers in implementing evidence-based practices.

Maegan Lokteff, Ph.D., has over 20 years working with children and families as an early childhood teacher, case manager, and administrator in for-profit and non-profit organizations. Since completing her Ph.D. in Family and Human Development from Utah State University, she serves as the Executive Director of Grand Beginnings, a nonprofit that supports early care and education programs and promotes child health and well-being in Rural Colorado.

Arlene R. Martin, Ed.D. in Curriculum and Teaching, was an Associate Professor in the Department of Early Childhood & Family Studies and former Director of Professional Impact NJ at Kean University of New Jersey. Her research interests and publications supported the field on mentoring adults, teacher education and leadership development.

Hedda Meadan, Ph.D., is an Associate Professor at the Department of Special Education at the University of Illinois, a Goldstick Family Scholar, a University Scholar, and a Board Certified Behavior Analyst. Dr. Meadan's areas of interest include social-communication skills and challenging behavior of individuals with autism and other developmental disabilities and intervention methods to enhance these spheres of functioning.

Deborah F. Perry, Ph.D., is the Director of Research and Evaluation and a professor at the Georgetown University Center for Child and Human

Development. Dr. Perry's research focuses on approaches to designing and testing preventive interventions for low-income young children and their caregivers. She has helped establish the evidence base for the effectiveness of Early Childhood Mental Health Consultation (ECMHC) in early childhood settings. She has co-authored more than a dozen peer-reviewed papers on ECMHC and has served as the principal investigator for 4 evaluations of ECMHC in Maryland and Washington DC over the last 15 years.

Rachel Pess, Psy.D., (married Gross) is a licensed psychologist who works at Stress and Anxiety Services of New Jersey. Dr. Pess specializes in the treatment of obsessive-compulsive disorder and anxiety disorders in children, adolescents, and adults utilizing cognitive behavioral therapy and exposure and response prevention. She is also an adjunct professor at Kean University.

Nicolette Rittenhouse-Young, Psy.D., is a psychologist who shares her time working in both the school and private practice settings. She has dedicated her career to helping individuals working through difficult issues, such as: anxiety, depression, attention/impulsivity difficulties, aggressive behavior, trauma, effective parenting, and substance use. Her passion is serving at-risk and adjudicated youth with a focus on utilizing positive behavior supports and unconditional positive regard as a means of building confidence, purpose, and prosocial behavior. She has a Doctorate in Clinical and School Psychology and a Masters in Educational Psychology from Kean University. She is currently director of Daytop Academy, a New Jersey state approved private special education school serving adolescents with substance use and cooccurring disorders.

Eva Marie Shivers, J.D., Ph.D. is the executive director of Indigo Cultural Center, a non-profit action research firm located in Phoenix, AZ. Dr. Shivers' research focuses on the developmental niche of early childhood development and education to explore the evolution of frameworks for understanding families' culturally adaptive responses to poverty, systemic racism, and historical marginalization. Dr. Shivers' work focuses on racial equity, teacher-child attachment in child care, mental health consultation,

List of Contributors

and evaluations of professional development initiatives. She currently provides racial equity training and consultation to early childhood community agencies and state departments around the country.

Rebecca N. Thomson received her Ph.D. in School Psychology from Michigan State University in 2018. She is currently completing a post-doctoral fellowship at Thriving Minds Family Services in Chelsea, MI. Her research focuses on evidence-based mental health interventions and ways in which access to these needed services can be increased for at-risk families.

Perspectives on
Early Childhood Psychology and Education

PECPE publishes twice a year, in the fall and spring. These two issues on specific focuses are typically guest-edited and can also include a few general articles.

Editorial Policy and Submission Guidelines

Perspectives on Early Childhood Psychology and Education focuses on publishing original contributions from a broad range of psychological and educational perspectives relevant to infants, young children (to age 8 years), families, and caregivers. Manuscripts incorporating evidence-based research, theory, and practice within clinical, community, developmental, neurological, and school psychology perspectives are considered. In addition, the journal accepts test and book reviews, literature reviews, program descriptions and evaluations, clinical studies, and other professional materials of interest to psychologists and educators working with young children. Proposals for special focus topics may be made to the Editor.

Format: Manuscripts should be original work not currently submitted for publication to other journals. Authors must follow the guidelines of the *Publication Manual of the American Psychological Association* (Sixth Edition). Manuscripts may not exceed 35 double-spaced pages in length, including the cover page, abstract, references, tables, and figures.

Submission: Submit an electronic copy of the manuscript for editorial review. Avoid including any identifying author information in the text. Selection of manuscripts is based on blind peer review. Include a cover page with the following information: the title of article, author(s) full name(s), title(s), institution or professional affiliations, and mailing and email address of primary author. The cover page will not be sent to reviewers.

Editorial Policy

Selection Criteria:

- Importance of topic in early childhood psychology and education
- Theory and research related to content
- Contribution to professional practice in early childhood psychology and education
- Clear and concise writing

CALL FOR PAPERS

We are seeking a special focus for the Spring 2019 issue of *PECPE*. If you are interested in submitting a topic and being the guest editor, please send a brief (approximately 250 words) proposal to Dr. David McIntosh, Editor-elect, *PECPE*: demcintosh@bsu.edu.

Special focus and general manuscripts for the Spring 2019 issue are due December 28, 2018. Manuscripts should be original work not currently submitted for publication to other journals. Authors must follow the guidelines of the *Publication Manual of the American Psychological Association* (Sixth Edition). Manuscripts may not exceed 35 double-spaced pages in length, including the cover page, abstract, references, tables, and figures. Avoid including any identifying author information in the text. Selection of manuscripts is based on blind peer review. Include a cover page with the following information: the title of article, author(s) full name(s), title(s), institution or professional affiliations, and mailing and email address of primary author. The cover page will not be sent to reviewers.

Volume 3, Issue 2 of
Perspectives on Early Childhood Psychology and Education
was published in Fall 2018
by Pace University Press

Cover and Interior Design by Sara Yager
Cover and Interior Layout by Jessica Estrella and Alicia Hughes
The journal was typeset in Minion and Myriad
and printed by Lightning Source

Pace University Press

Director: Manuela Soares
Associate Director: Stephanie Hsu
Marketing Manager: Patricia Hinds
Design Consultant: Sara Yager

Graduate Assistants: Jessica Estrella and Alicia Hughes
Student Aide: Erica Magrin

www.ingramcontent.com/pod-product-compliance
Lightning Source LLC
Chambersburg PA
CBHW061445300426
44114CB00014B/1849